Luke's Daughters

A Memoir of Northfork, West Virginia

Jenna Gianato Calovini
Martha Gianato Rector

Some names have been changed and/or individuals mentioned are composite characters

Unless otherwise identified, all photographs are from the Gianato Family Collection

Contact authors: lukesdaughters@yahoo.com

Copyright © 2013 Jenna Gianato Calovini & Martha Gianato Rector
All rights reserved.
ISBN: 1481123831
ISBN 13: 9781481123839
Library of Congress Control Number: 2012922844
CreateSpace Independent Publishing Platform
North Charleston, South Carolina

For Luke's Granddaughters
Laura and Jennifer

Note from the Authors

Dear Readers,

Several years ago as we drove through Northfork, West Virginia on a family visit, we were so surprised at the changes to our hometown, the condition of many houses and buildings we knew well, and the abandoned school we so loved. Casually we said we wished our daughters could understand what Northfork and those times were like when we grew up. As the months progressed, we decided to record some memories so they and future generations could appreciate our roots. As we delved into the project and through all the wonderful mementos Mother had saved, the snapshot we envisioned became a pretty large portrait.

It is important to note that each chapter is its own short story about family, neighbors, friends, or the times. The memoir features home life, educational development, the effects of national and local political events, and the influences of television and music. We girls also experienced the segregation and slow integration of the races, work and social values, and religion. As anchors in the memoir, the fleeting impressions and the people around us helped shape us and our memories. References to ethnic groups such as Italians or African-Americans are reflective of the habits and customs of the times in that small-town environment in Appalachia during the 1950s and 1960s.

Another dynamic of the portrait throughout much of the memoir features the five-year age difference of us two sisters. This five-year span influenced our activities and behaviors, our outlooks, and how we viewed life. Our goal has been a humorous, positive look at the West Virginia coalfields rather than a negative look at the people of Appalachia.

What follows is that full portrait, colored by our memories and frozen moments in time.

Love,
Jenna Lou and Martha

Chapter 1

Big Fish, Little Fish

Growing up in southern West Virginia in the '50s and '60s meant one thing to me: the nurturing of a vivid imagination. I remember I was always living in the future, both short term (when I get to junior high) and long term (high school, the prom, my wedding day). I guess I was unusual as I wanted to go away to some boarding school—my Jackie Kennedy influence. Living through others was a big deal too: movie stars, television stars, and my sister. I was always on the go and in every school activity so I could please my mother. Getting as many pictures as possible in the yearbook was important, but I was always still thinking ahead or looking behind. Living for the day was not an option, or even considered. It would be many years before I could appreciate living for the day, let alone appreciate my dad's upward mobility and the beautiful mountains of my youth.

It has been said that there were four acres of coal underground in McDowell County for every acre aboveground. Coal was the industry—no tourism, no ATVs, no skiing. It was the million-dollar coalfields, and all ethnic groups from mostly Europe came to get a job. It was actually a diverse culture, with many of the groups assimilating as quickly as possible to become Americans and live the American dream. The old-timers still spoke their native language with the second and third generations trying to become as "WASP" as possible. If an ethnic from eastern or southern Europe married someone of the English, German, Irish, or French descent, they married up. Such was the case of my dad, Luke Gianato. Both of his parents came to America from Italy and met here.

A couple of years after my dad's death in the late 1990s, I remembered a conversation we had one afternoon while standing in his automobile showroom in Northfork, West Virginia. It was in the late 1950s, and I was really at the height of my boredom. It was late in the day, and the sun was going behind the high mountains with just specks of dust filling the air in its reflection. The floor had a squared pattern, and the room was big enough for one of those big, four-door Pontiacs with the long taillights. I was leaning against the big Pontiac Firechief model, and Dad had on his checkered sport coat and dress pants. He was dialing up the combination to the black safe that stood along one wall of the dealership. It was a big safe. So big that in order to open the door—once the combination was completed—Dad had to pull open the door and swing it way out using all his weight to do so. As usual, I was talking, and asked him the following question, "Daddy, are we big fish in a little sea or little fish in a big sea?" He replied, "I guess we are big fish in a little sea." We did have more than most in the coal-mining Appalachian Mountains, living in a brick house and going to Myrtle Beach on vacation every summer when most lived in coal-company, wood houses. I then said, "I want to be a big fish in a big sea." He said, "That is very hard to do; and as a girl, you have to marry a big fish to be a big fish." It was then I thought about getting out of the coalfields, going to some place like Washington, DC, New York City, or Hollywood to be a big fish. I did agree it would be easier to marry a big fish, but I didn't know any big-fish boys, and I wanted to marry for love, not money. After all, Daddy said we'd never have to worry about money. I really never thought about being a big fish on my own. It was before women's lib.

The odds of my being here were slim to none. My mother was six-and one-half months along when I decided to enter the world. Of course her Kool cigarettes, Cokes, and lack of vitamins may have had something to do with it. The story goes that it was snowing in early December 1946. Daddy was playing cards at the "Snafu," a joint he co-owned. The phones were out, and I was ready to be born. Eventually Daddy came home and got Mother to the hospital. Daddy used to say I was so small he could hold me in the palm of his hand. I was supposed to die, but Dr. Villani put me in an incubator. Place: Welch, West Virginia. I was named Jenny Lou Gianato, after my mother (Jenny) and her sister (Louise). Against all odds, I lived and came home in early 1947. I guess Mother only wanted one Jenny around, so I became Jenna, and was called Jenna Lou from grade school through high school. I wanted to be Beverly, Peggy, Kathy, or Pamela. Nobody had a name like mine. I was the smallest and the skinniest, or so I was told constantly. Some people called me Skinny Lou, Jensy Lucy, Lulu, and don't forget the sophisticated Jemper Lou. Right from the start, self-image was a major influence on me, and what other people thought was paramount. Not until I was in my thirties did I ever hear of another Jenna, which is now quite a common name. Mother dressed me very well, and with my pigtails, big eyes, and big mouth, I was a hoot. Even when I was very young, I was bored. I carried a deck of cards with a rubber band around it, bugging everybody to play with me. Perhaps my penchant for games of chance and risk-taking began then. I would sing and dance at the drop of a hat, and did quite a bit of entertaining when company came. Naturally I wanted to be a movie star or a secretary from ages five through fourteen.

I was also very gullible. I used to ask, "Where did I come from?" The answer was always, "You were hatched from an egg that was dropped by the stork behind the colored church." That was the extent of my sex education, seriously. It was the same with anything scientific—Daddy told me there was a man in the moon, and the moon was made of green cheese. It didn't make any sense, but if he said it was so, it was.

Having the name Jenna Lou Gianato in Appalachia may be a clue to my restlessness. The last name was pronounced "Jeanette," like the girl's name. All locals knew how to pronounce it, especially since all the radio commercials for the dealership pronounced it "Jeanette." Over the years I have been known as Jenna Lou, Jenna, Jenna Harris, and Jenna Calovini. Maybe I just keep reinventing myself and haven't realized it. But when I think back to my early years at home, my sister and I were known around town—and we proudly defined ourselves—as "Luke's Daughters."

CHAPTER 2

Drawer B

McDowell (pronounced MAC-Dowell by the locals) County, West Virginia, is in the heart of Appalachia. When people make West Virginia jokes, any native-born West Virginian really wants to punch them in the face. However, folks from Charleston, Morgantown, or Martinsburg think of the stereotypical hicks of West Virginia as those from McDowell County, not them. Folks from Chester and Newell in the northern part of the state even call all of us living south of Wheeling, "Whoopies," a term given to those ignorant hillbillies who could only get work making hoops for the pottery barrels years ago. Yet the proud folks from McDowell County are in denial of it all. Yes, there was lots of poverty, hardship, and ignorance; but there was also civility, good manners, hardworking people, and pride.

Our hometown was Northfork, West Virginia, right on Route 52, as opposed to up the hollers. We lived in the Elkridge addition. In later years, I can't count the number of times when I mentioned my hometown was Northfork, West Virginia, and people thought I meant Norfolk, Virginia. Of course all of us locals pronounced Northfork without accentuating the "th," so it was easy for anyone to be confused. Between explaining my last name, "Jeanette," and the hometown of Northfork, I had a lot of good introductory conversations while smoking cigarettes and having cocktails. The most common follow-up to "Northfork", not "Norfolk" was "What's your address?" My honest answer was always "Drawer B, Northfork, West Virginia." Most really belly laughed when I said the Drawer B address bit. Since we didn't have street names and the hub of the town was the post office, we used Daddy's car dealership post-office box as our address.

One of my favorite games was to have some real smart guy who was trying to impress me guess how to pronounce my last name. I would bet them fifty dollars, spell G-I-A-N-A-T-O, and they would say "Giant-o" or "Gee-i-nato." I always won. Then I would explain that when my grandfather got his shipments at the railroad station in Kimball for his grocery store, the stationmaster couldn't pronounce "Giannattisio," the original name in Italian. So the stationmaster shortened it to Gianato. My granddad, in his broken English, would say his name was "Jimmy Jenett," and so there you go. It has been said my grandfather's grocery store in Kimball, begun in 1921, did well. Daddy always told us girls what a stern taskmaster he was, and how he expected our dad to work in the store, even as a young boy. Daddy told us that he and his cronies would slip away during the day to shoot "craps" behind the Kimball Post Office, throwing the dice up against the back post-office wall. He would even hear his father yelling for him to come to work, but ignored his calls. Time and again Grandfather would stomp up the hill, grab Daddy by the ear, and march him back to the store. Daddy would always add that Grandfather could really pull hard at that ear to make a point, but that never kept Daddy from shooting "craps" again with the gang.

Daddy also described Grandfather as rather short, but extremely strong and powerfully built. He could carry two twenty-pound bags of flour on each shoulder, and climb any hill or steps to deliver his goods to customers. He was doing exactly this when his grocery-delivery truck got caught in cold, early-spring waters trying to cross a swollen creek in Superior. Standing in the cold water, he helped a family stranded in the floodwaters get to safety. Sick, he died within a week of pneumonia, never seeing his son—our dad—succeed. Daddy always said Grandfather wanted him to become a lawyer. That was a pretty big dream since Italians in southern West Virginia weren't lawyers at that time. In fact, Italians were often treated as second-class citizens along with all the immigrants from Eastern Europe who came to work the coalfields. To accentuate their lower-class standing, Italians were commonly called Tally, Wops, or Dagos.

Chapter 3

About Luke and Jenny

Daddy quit high school and worked awhile, then went back to school and graduated. He was very intelligent and could solve algebra problems in his head, and had a most dynamic personality. He could sell anybody, anything, at any time. He loved to sell. Young and old, men and women all really liked him. In the early years he had a restaurant that had slot machines in the back, a men's clothing store, and then moved on to his love—selling cars. When he finally got his own dealership, he expanded it through the years and was in business over thirty-five years. That's really good for a small area where repeat business is a necessity. His business had a good reputation, thanks to all the good, hardworking employees he had. I can remember Sunday afternoons, Christmas Eves, birthdays, and vacations put on hold to "make a deal." I always wanted a normal household with quitting time and payday, like my friends. I had a love/hate relationship with Daddy's work. We reaped the benefits, but we had no predictable time with him. Daddy had the most wonderful signature. The way he would loop the "L" in Luke and the "G" in Gianato was big, bold, and daring—like him. Luke Gianato was the type who just took over the room when he entered. Daddy was a businessman—not the fix-it-up type—so we always had workmen do electrical, plumbing, or carpentry work. His hands were big and soft, just perfect for a little girl to grasp.

Whenever I got in trouble, Daddy would say, "I see you are in hot water again!" Daddy had a temper, but I knew he was all show. He didn't spank us, Mother did. I would ask Daddy for a spanking instead of having to listen to his lectures and drawn out explanations. As a young, Italian man, he lived by his wits and good luck, but worked very hard and "married up." If an Italian man could marry a "pie-eater," WASP, his social status was enhanced. Remember Italians and other immigrants from Eastern Europe were on the lower rung of the social ladder, just above the "colored" in early twentieth-century McDowell County.

Mother, who was the only one of her family to graduate high school, took care of the household bills and wrote the checks. Mother also drove her car when many women didn't even have one, and would drive us to faraway places such as Washington, PA and Myrtle Beach. A careful and skillful driver, Mother was our first seat belt. Any sudden stop or fast slowdown, and out came her right arm—rigid and straight—to hold one of us girls safely in place in the front seat. She was creative at decorating, but Mother knew when anything had been moved or touched inappropriately anywhere in the house. We, therefore, worked around what she wanted and how she wanted it, much like other areas of our lives with her in the years to come.

Mother's family had a big, coal-company house, one of the first cars in Vivian Bottom, a telephone, a pony, and lots of food from the garden—even in the Great Depression. Her dad, Edgar Cooke, had an important job at the coal mines in Vivian, supervising the boiler and heating system for the coal mines, the company store, and all the houses in the local coal camps of Peerless and Vivian. Their home place was nicely decorated with stylish furniture, including a player piano, and a sunroom with one glass wall that held an extensive salt-and pepper-shake collection. The house was a very popular hangout place for the local teenagers and for Mother, her two brothers, and two sisters. Many Saturday nights the rugs would be rolled back, and the kids would play the radio or the piano and dance their hearts out.

My sister was born four years into my parents' marriage and was named Martha, after our grandmother. In 1943, Daddy enlisted in the army's infantry, and fought mostly in Germany. Martha at that time was two years old. Daddy's three brothers were also war veterans, all proud Americans, doing much for McDowell County veterans' activities throughout the following years. The family grocery store has been in Kimball about 100 years.

With Daddy overseas, Mother and Martha moved back to Vivian to stay at her childhood home. One time Mother took the train to Washington, DC, to see Daddy before he shipped out overseas. I think after this experience on the "troop train" that her love for travel ceased. She was surrounded by all those soldiers who whistled and catcalled out to her. Mother always said she "was scared to death!" The train conductor sat her next to him, and there she sat all the way to Washington, DC.

Months later—on February 6, 1944, to be exact—Mr. Payne, Kimball's telegraph office manager, knocked on their door in Vivian. Just seeing Mr. Payne standing on a porch during the war would put the fear of doom in every heart, since a telegram always meant bad news. He read the telegram to Mother. "The U.S. Army regrets to inform you that Luke A. Gianato was wounded in action Twenty January in Germany," he said, and then handed the telegram to Mother. Three-year-old Martha, standing close by, starting crying and screamed out, "Those damn Germans shot my daddy!"

Daddy also had a story he told about that incident. The story goes that after he was shot, he was left behind to wait for the medics. Along came a jeep, decorated with numerous stars, which immediately stopped in front of Daddy. Out jumps General George S. Patton. He demanded to know why Daddy was not with his outfit and why he didn't salute. After Daddy explained he had been shot in his arm and was waiting for transport to the behind-the-lines field hospital, General Patton then saluted him and told him to "carry on." Dad was awarded the Purple Heart for his wound. Many years later, Daddy showed us the scar on his arm from that injury.

After Dad recovered from his injury, he went back into combat. It was during that time he was awarded the Bronze Star for "outstanding courage and devotion to duty, under fire." While capturing several German patrol members, he obtained information that helped to ensure the entire German patrol was killed or captured. Dad's actions also prevented casualties among the members of his army unit. He didn't take advantage of the GI Bill, but for the rest of his life he received thirteen dollars a month from the government because his feet were frozen during the harsh, European winters.

Following General Patton's war command to "carry on," Daddy did just that on the troop ship, the Queen Mary, heading home to the United States. He won hundreds of dollars playing cards, which was a great start for them after the war. With Daddy home, Martha remembers walking with him in his uniform, his big, soft hand holding hers. Kimball streets were crowded sidewalk to street with all the army, navy, and marines finally home. Everyone greeted him on the street, and all were happy he made it home safely. It was a loud, happy celebration, scary for a little four-year-old. The celebration moved into the East End Cafe, Daddy's restaurant, where he sat Martha on a counter to keep her out of the way. Daddy went with his war buddies into the back to shoot a game of pool, and Martha clearly remembers studying all the details of the big pickle jar on the counter right beside her.

I was born in the very first wave of baby boomers, so we were a family of four. I was a pain to my sister and knew it. But I loved being a pest, probably because of boredom. Being five years younger, my sister thought I was always at the wrong place at the wrong time. I wanted to be like her so much.

CHAPTER 4

Skinny Little Tally Boy

Mother's mother was born in 1893. This special woman was the light of both our lives. I nicknamed her Remmie, after Uncle Remus in the funny paper. (We never called them comics.) Every Sunday she would read the funnies to Martha and me, acting out the characters. Her best voice was Uncle Remus. I loved this so much I started calling her Remus, then gave it a feminine touch, Remmie. The name stuck. So thanks to a four-year-old, this wonderful, loving, nurturing, positive woman with the strong name of Martha Ellen, was forever known as Remmie. As my mother and her siblings were growing up, my grandmother was a rock in the community and was very charitable to anyone in the coal camp. In fact, Remmie said that Uncle Lewis (Mother's oldest brother) would let Daddy tag along with him. He would bring Daddy home so Remmie could feed that "skinny little Tally boy." Since Mother was always around, Dad took notice of her, and the rest is history. Mom always said Daddy married her because of Remmie's cooking! When I asked Daddy what Mother was like when she was young, he said most affectionately: "Jenny Cooke was the prettiest girl I ever saw. I pestered her long enough that she finally gave in!" Daddy forever loved Remmie and was her Rock of Gibraltar as she aged. Remmie loved Daddy and always considered him as another son.

A 1940s women's libber, Remmie left Mother to manage her household and went to Elkton, Maryland, to work in a munitions factory to help the World War II effort. Three silver stars hung from her window to depict three family members in the service. Daddy was in the army in Europe, Uncle Lewis in the navy based out of Jacksonville, FL, and Uncle Junior was in the navy serving in the Pacific. Most men in McDowell County were serving somewhere overseas or helping the war effort by working in the coal mines. As the war wound down, Remmie returned to Vivian, proud of her own war efforts. It has been said and proven—based on population percentages—that West Virginia provided the highest number of military personnel during World War II than any other state in the country. Remmie was very, very patriotic and very vocal about her political views.

My grandfather, Ed, died in 1947. Coal company rules dictated that when the company employee died, the family had to move from the house the coal company provided. Remmie broke up housekeeping, sending all of her belongings around to her children. From that point forward, she would spend time with each of her children. She stayed with us quite regularly, and sometimes for long periods. We got her multi-piece bedroom suite, which would forever stay with us. Pieces of that bedroom suite are still with Martha and my daughter, Jennifer. The big mystery through all the years was what happened to Remmie's big collection of salt-and-pepper shakers. On occasion she would talk about them, and through the years I asked Mother where they were because they meant so much to Remmie. Mother would say, "They got lost." Well, the mystery was solved in 2007, while we were preparing my mother's house for sale in Welch. After days of going through countless boxes and stacks of paper—and looking at every item Mother ever saved—I came across a nondescript box in the furnace room. I opened the box and lifted out the first item. Low and behold, it was a set of salt-and-pepper shakers shaped like sail boats. Bursting into tears, I immediately called Martha. The 1947 *Bluefield Daily Telegraph* newspaper wrapped around each set of shakers proved they had not been touched since they were wrapped up sixty years before. It was like unwrapping gold to me, and each one felt quite sacred in my hands. I treasured opening each one!

Some of our most exciting times growing up was when Remmie would come home to stay—riding on the Greyhound bus from Florida or Georgia—and we would pick her up in Bluefield, twenty miles away. Getting to the bus station very early, we would look over the magazines and toys, and wait, and wait. The bus was never on time. We would jump up and down when we saw her coming down those steps off the bus. After we got her bags, we would go into the bus station dining room and have a plate dinner or a hamburger. Remmie traveled quite often, going both north and south, so it seemed we were going to Bluefield more often than not.

Remmie was a crocheter, and I would sit and watch her work. I was too impatient to learn how to crochet myself, but Martha did learn to some degree. We still have many of her crocheted items and treasure them. She talked a lot about sewing, and always studied the sewing patterns from the newspaper. Those sewing patterns were located right by the horoscopes. Remmie would read "her fortune" and memorize the patterns, just in case she decided to make something special. I particularly liked to watch Remmie sew with her thimble when she was mending or sewing up something special. All her sewing was hand stitched, no machine. A woman's success story during those times depended on being known as a good housekeeper, a good cook, a good seamstress, and a valuable volunteer in the community. Remmie met all those criteria.

Mother's oldest sister, Gladys, was really beautiful. She wore just the best clothes, had her nails done at the beauty shop, and was a "business" woman. She talked business, drank bourbon, smoked Herbert Taryetons, and had a great laugh. While she was a good cook and did sewing, she didn't talk about it. From her I learned there was more to life than "keeping house." I thought she was the most interesting woman, as opposed to the traditional kind of wife. The last thing I ever wanted to do was to clean, cook, or sew.

Mother's second sister, Louise, had a big family, played the piano "by heart," and danced up a jig. I loved all seven cousins—from Norma, the oldest, to Jenny Lee, the youngest. Cousin Norma joined the service and eventually married an Air Force Captain. Cousin Shirley loved to dance and taught us kids the latest dance steps. At age seventeen, Cousin Buddy enlisted in the air force. I was especially close to Jackie and Sharon, both nearer my age. Martha and her favorite cousin, Ronda Gay, were the same age and always seemed close. Ronda was a fragile girl—a sweetie, a lot of fun, but tired easily. Ill with a heart condition brought on by rheumatic fever, doctors advised Uncle Blaine and Aunt Louise that an operation may help improve her health. However her dad refused to give permission, saying it was too dangerous. Ronda died during her teen years, a sad and tragic time for all our families.

Another reason to go to Bluefield was Uncle Junior. I didn't see him a lot. He was a navy veteran, was as handsome as Paul Newman, loved the ladies, and never seemed to have any kind of real job. He was on the road a lot. He would call Mother, reversing the charges, and beg for money. Some people said he was a con artist, whatever that was. Mother and Daddy would confer, and they always sent the money. Uncle Junior created a routine for us. We would drive to Bluefield to the Western Union office, wire the money, and go to the bus station to eat. One time Junior called crying and crying. His "latest wife" had died. Explaining the whys and hows of her death, he then asked for money to bury her. Very concerned, Mother promptly agreed and went through the Western Union routine. Ten days later the telephone rang. It was a collect call from "Harriett Hussie," as Remmie called her—Uncle Junior's "dead wife." Mother couldn't believe her ears! "Harriett Hussie" was mad as a hornet. She was looking for Junior, and wanted to know where he was. In anger, Mother told "Harriett Hussie" in no uncertain terms, "If you ever find Junior, give him this message for me: Never call me again!" So in the early 1960s, those Western Union visits stopped. Uncle Junior did call, but from that point forward, he never asked for any more money.

Before Luke shipped out to Europe during World War II, Jenny visited him in Washington, DC.

Stylishly dressed, Remmie toured the Norfolk harbor during the 1940s.

Uncle Junior poses with Martha and Jenna Lou at the house in Northfork.

When Mother put on her fur piece, we girls knew we would be dressing up in our best. Daddy takes an Easter photo of Martha, Jenna Lou, and Jenny.

Chapter 5

Granny Nance Dipped Snuff

Remmie's mother, our great-grandmother, was Granny Nance. A short, stout woman, she had not one gray hair when she died. It was said she was one-fourth Cherokee and that was why we all had high cheekbones. Granny was nothing like Remmie, the tall, attractive grandmother we loved. Granny Nance—never called by her given name Joanna Frances—had a big bump on her tongue that showed every time she spoke. Besides that, she dipped snuff and spit into her "snuff can" at regular intervals. I don't think she dipped in church, though. It is no wonder she scared the bejesus out of me, as the saying went. I remember one time we went to visit her, and Remmie made me give Granny a kiss. I just wanted to die. All of her children would gather around her like she was royalty. The thing about Granny was that she was always moving her residence. She lived in at least five places that I can remember in a short time span. She hit every coal camp between Kimball and Northfork, some several times. She was also just a big gossip.

Granny called Remmie "Marthie" which irked me too. Granny was always talking about something being as wild as "Coxie's Army" and talked a lot about when President McKinley was shot. She was talking about her times, for sure. Perhaps I should have listened more closely! Mother didn't care for Granny; in fact, Mother would shake her head, roll her eyes, and say, "Granny Nance never gave me a hug or said a single nice thing to me, and she was my grandmother."

Granny's second husband was Jack Nance. He worked in the mines for years and years, and as a result, was permanently slumped over from bending down in the low-hanging coal of the mines. He waited on Granny hand and foot. One time Granny and Jack went to a tent revival meeting. By mistake, Granny put twenty dollars from her "bill folder" in the collection plate. She made Jack go back the next day and get her twenty dollars from that "thieving" preacher. Granny was always saying things like "I reckon," or "make hay while the sun shines," or "if the Lord's willing and the creek don't rise." The grossest thing she did in my opinion, and from a young child's perspective, was to dip her corn bread in her buttermilk. I have never been able to eat corn bread or drink buttermilk ever since.

One day Mother saw someone opening the gate that was at the top of the nineteen steep steps to the landing outside our house. Then she saw Jack Nance, all hunched over, start up the porch steps. Mother said, while pinching my arm, "Be quiet. Don't answer the door. It's Jack Nance trying to sell some Fuller brushes. I don't want to fool with him, and he probably doesn't have his teeth in." He knocked and knocked, and then slowly left. That was one I couldn't figure out.

In early summer of 1963, Remmie, Mother, Martha, and my niece Laura went to see Granny. They wanted a photo of five generations. During the visit, Granny said she was "going to see Jesus soon," and she insisted Martha take home her forty-year-old Christmas cactus. It was big, bulky, and ironically blooming. Martha finally agreed, barely squeezing the plant into the car. She carefully placed the plant by her side dining room window, but within six weeks the plant died, and so had Granny. I only saw Granny Nance wear black. But she was always talking about what "she was going to be laid out in." One time it was blue, and then it was pink. When she died and was "laid out" with all that black hair at the age of eighty-eight, she was buried in purple. Go figure.

Mother did have some interesting relatives who made an impression on Martha and me. Arlene Blevins was the wife of Mother's cousin, James Blevins. She was from Little Rock, Arkansas, and looked just like the singer Peggy Lee. Arlene was a yo-yo dieter before yo-yo dieting was even thought about. On many occasions, her weight was a topic of conversation. She even told us she lost all of her weight taking Epsom salts, or as Grant Blevins (her father-in-law) would say, "Arlene's done took to the Epsom Sauce." She carried around a Chihuahua, saying the dog had special powers to help cure her asthma. Not only that, but Arlene wore purple lipstick. All of that was pretty unusual for anyone in McDowell County in the 1950s. Of course, Martha and I thought she was really interesting, and she had a cute laugh. Mother would just roll her eyes.

One of Remmie's sisters was Nell. Nell was the youngest of the brood and lived in Philadelphia. She dressed very modern and was a bit prissy. Remmie always commented on Nell's fancy "earbobs," her earrings. When I was a teenager, I would always talk to her about *American Bandstand*, and she always invited me to come to Philadelphia so I could dance on TV. Of course, Mother said, "Absolutely not!" Mother never said why I couldn't.

CHAPTER 6

Big Four Starland Theatre

Sarah and Grant Blevins were Remmie's sister and brother-in-law. Grant, a World War I veteran, was a coal miner. Sarah—Sarie, as Grant called her—had long, long hair, which she usually wore in a bun. She had false teeth but didn't always wear them. She had those high cheekbones like Remmie, and was very tall. They lived on the exit side of the Starland Drive-In Theatre in Big Four. In fact, they were the first house at the exit. The Starland sat right on top of the mountain, but was only open from Memorial Day to Labor Day due to the cold weather the rest of the year. Grant knew all the movies because he would walk past his outhouse, up a small incline, sit on some rocks, and watch the movies. Some of his favorites were *Red River Valley*, *Sergeant York*, and *Popeye* cartoons. You could hear the sound of the movies echoing from their front porch too. If we went to visit, we had to leave before the movie was over because of all the traffic congestion, but mostly because of the unpaved, exit road. It was all dirt, and with the cars moving bumper-to-bumper, the dust flew everywhere. It was a hot mess. I can still hear Mother yelling, "Hurry up, hurry up, we got to go—the movie is letting out!" When the movie was over, the big flood lights above the screen came on, lighting up the sky and shining into Sarah's kitchen. Then an announcement would be made that boomed across the mountaintop. "Thank you for visiting the Starland Drive-In Theatre. Please put the speaker back on the post. Come again soon."

One time—for some unknown reason—we spent the night at Sarah and Grant's. The house was very cold. But the scary part for us as young girls was the big picture of Jesus on one side of the fireplace ledge and the picture of their son, Charles, on the other side. Charles was killed in an automobile accident, and somehow the combination of the two scared us—especially since Sarie didn't keep lights on at night like we did. It was pitch black. We heard strange, scary sounds, and we huddled together whispering to each other. "Was that Charles or was that Jesus?" we wondered. The worst part was going to the bathroom at the outhouse. Of course as soon as we got in bed, we had to go; then Grant had to shine his flashlight so we could find our way. In the morning Sarah baked homemade biscuits, but they were hard as nails on the outside and gooey on the inside. These two were fun, said and did silly things, and we did just love being around them. Sarah and Grant were very special people in our lives.

CHAPTER 7

Sleeping at "The Woodlawn"

We went to the cemetery often, and always on "Decoration Day," now called Memorial Day, Easter, and Christmas. Every family member and in-law got fresh flowers put on their graves, with Aunt Gladys helping with the expense. When we got to my grandfather's grave, Remmie would say, "Here is where I will be, next to Ed." When I was really young, I remember Remmie talking about Ed "being asleep" up at Woodlawn. I could never figure out why he had to sleep there.

I remember my first experience with death. Aunt Gladys' husband, Ferris Pettit—Uncle Tom to us—was killed in the mines. A tall, handsome man, they had been married for at least fifteen years when he was killed by a runaway, underground coal car. It was the custom then to have the wake at a home, not a funeral parlor. Since our house was large, the wake was held at ours. Mother even took down the dining room table to make room for all the visitors. I was too short to see into the casket, so Remmie picked me up and held me so I could see. Because Uncle Tom had such severe injuries, there was a thin, see-through net over the top of the casket so the body was visible but not entirely exposed. Remmie told me to touch the body, but I was too scared. The visitations lasted several days. The casket would be closed late night and early day, only opened when visitations started. All afternoon and evening folks came to visit, brought food, and sat. All of this really made an impression on me, but I wasn't too disturbed by the whole thing since the grown-ups acted like this was just natural. Uncle Tom was buried at Woodlawn Cemetery, on the hill not far from Remmie and her Ed. All of Daddy's family are at Woodlawn and are joined now by Daddy and Mother. In fact, just about everyone we have ever loved is buried at Woodlawn.

In later years, Woodlawn installed a multicolored waterfall that lit up at night in front of the new mausoleums. So at night we would drive up Route 52, park on the side of the road, and watch the waterfall change colors. It didn't take much to entertain us.

CHAPTER 8

Northfork, WV, not Norfolk, VA

McDowell County during most of the twentieth century was known as "The Nation's Coal Bin." When coal was king, towns in the coalfields were busy and bustling. In lean years, coal miners might work two or three shifts a week, maybe only one shift a week if times were really tough. But the 1950s and early 1960s, for the most part, saw little towns like Northfork benefiting from the profits of "King Coal."

It was during our school days in Northfork that we could always be proud of our little town. The streets were clean, and a variety of businesses filled every store along Main Street. The continuous row of willow trees that stretched along the entire left side of the road from Dead Man's Cut to the stoplight at the middle of town were a stately sight that set Northfork apart from any other town in McDowell (remember, that's MAC-Dowell) County.

Driving though Northfork was like threading a needle. The two-lane road was squeezed between two mountains, Elkhorn Creek, and the N&W Railroad. Any building not on the roadside was either across the creek and the railroad track or sitting up high on the side of the mountain. It was usually difficult to find a parking spot along Main

Street since parking in town had a pattern. Heading toward Bluefield, the parking along the street was parallel, with parking meters at each spot. A nickel would get you thirty minutes. Across the street, was pull-in parking at an angle. Many times drivers would drive through town, not find a parking spot, turn around at the Curb-In restaurant, and try again. Or if you headed in the opposite direction, the turnaround was in the back alley behind the jail.

While we always called this main drag Main Street or just "town," this road, which went through all the small towns of Northfork, Keystone, Kimball, Big Four, and on into Welch, was U.S. Route 52. It stretched from the Great Lakes to the Deep South. What always amazed Martha and me was this very exact road that ran through our town and our lives every single day was also the exact road that took us toward Myrtle Beach. These two ends of Rt. 52 have kept us connected in many ways our entire lives.

Coming into town from Keystone was a line of stores, businesses, and houses all grouped together like most small towns. First came the Church of God and then the Appalachian Subpower Station, where if you saw a large number of power trucks you knew that the power was off in some part of town. Next sat the Curb-In and a row of attached houses that we called "the apartments," now known as townhomes. Among the neighbors were Mr. Bennett, the funeral home owner and his wife; Betty Lodolo, our Physical Education teacher and her husband; Dr. and Mrs. Riffe, the dentist, and their son Bob. The liquor store, McDowell Floral— where we ordered all our funeral flowers—and The Western Auto were all "down the street." Among the stores lined up along the street were Tomchin's Furniture, the "Hole-in-the-Wall" eatery, Kroger's, Sam Arena's Shoe Shop, A&P, the old post office, G.C. Murphy's, the drugstore, Edna's Ladies Shop, hardware stores, and a loan office on the corner to name a few. Above all these stores were apartments filled with individuals and families.

The corner created the main intersection in town, which also had THE one traffic light in town. One left turn and you crossed the bridge over Elkhorn Creek to the train depot. A right turn took you by the old Linda's Beauty Shop, the cabstand, and City Hall, which had one jail cell in the back. Go pay your water bill, and you could check out any prisoner being held for the state police. Most important for us girls was Daddy's Pontiac dealership located at this exact intersection. His showroom faced Rt. 52, and the new and used car lot sat along the side street across from City Hall. Throw in lawyers, doctors, gas stations, and a land company, and Northfork was quite a nice community.

Heading toward Bluefield from the front door of Daddy's dealership, you walked past the pool hall, Hartell's Insurance, and Williams' Tri-District Cleaners. Crossing the street, you were at Carroll's Motor Sales, which sold Chevrolets, Oldsmobiles, and Cadillacs. Tucked behind Carroll's auto bay was the Freeman Theatre. The Masonic Lodge and the First Methodist Church stood side by side next to the grade school and high school building, with Mahaffey's next door.

Heading out of Northfork were houses on both sides of the road, all mostly brick. Most everyone in town could close their eyes and name the people who lived in every house along this part of town, as well as those who lived on Clark Hill, the residential area that sat behind most of the town, just it was up on the hill. Some houses on Clark Hill went as high up the hill as the town's water tower. Now that was really high up the hill, but what a view! If there weren't leaves on the trees, you could see all the way to Algoma, probably a mile or more away as the crow flies. Heaven forbid if a winter snowstorm hit unexpectedly and caught cars parked on the hill. Attempting to maneuver down the hill and around the corner could cause major anxiety to even the most experienced driver. However, walking was an easy task in Northfork since concrete sidewalks ran from Dead Man's Cut at one end of town to the bottom of Kyle Hill on the other end, exactly one mile. We walked from one place to another as a means of transportation through town. No one ever thought of walking as exercise.

During our time in Northfork, all the stores closed every day at five o'clock. The bank was closed on Saturday, and there were no ATMs. Drive-through windows at the bank came much later to Northfork. Nothing was open on Sunday except a few local restaurants, which only opened after church. Aside from Sunday, you could buy most anything you needed or wanted—from ice cream and caskets to clothes and furniture. You could catch a train, a bus, or Mr. Cornett's cab. Houses were big, small, and in between made of brick, wood, or combinations of the two. Mansions dotted our area from the coal barons' era. One such "biggy" was the Beury Mansion in Algoma, with its ballroom, bowling alley, and chauffeur who drove the family dog around each morning. With little flat land, houses "grew up" the mountainsides; these are now called chateaus. I can never remember an empty house in our part of the world. Northfork had its own water system, known area-wide to have the "best water" around. Our police force consisted of a chief and one policeman. The Northfork Volunteer Fire Department also supported Elkridge, Algoma, Gilliam, Indian Ridge, Ashland, and Crumpler when any fire happened.

Now the drugstore and my big mouth got me in real hot water with Mother one day. Mother, Martha, and I were sitting on the high stools at the soda counter sipping Cokes and munching on fresh cookies. Bored with this, I started twisting side to side on my stool and singing, "Today my mother is forty-five years old, forty-five years, forty-five years old." I just kept on singing and being quite annoying. Mother, while pinching me on the arm, tried hushing me up, but I just kept singing louder.

Totally fed up, Mother pulled me off my stool, grabbed Martha, and shoved us out the door. Angry beyond words, Mother gritted her teeth saying, "I'll have you know, I am forty!"

Of all the buildings in Northfork, the most unique was the "Hole in the Wall" restaurant, formally known as the Central Quick Lunch. Just imagine seventy inches wide and ninety feet long, the eatery was created when a roof was constructed over an alley between two buildings. Always crowded, I only knew that men went in there for its famous liver and onion sandwiches.

The four white churches around Northfork included Baptist, Methodist, and Presbyterian, all within walking distance of each other. The Church of God was on the lower end of town. The Catholic Church was several miles up the road in Powhatan, pronounced "Pow-tan." The colored churches were scattered, but mostly in the little coal camps. We even heard there were churches in the far reaches of the county that "handled snakes," but those folks were really back in the hollers. Everyone in the Northfork area—white and colored—dressed up for church, which meant hats and gloves for women and girls on most occasions. Men always wore suits or coats, shirts, and ties. Kids wore their best to church, whatever their best was.

Besides church, a "quasi" social event was when the Bennett Funeral Home had a viewing of a deceased townsperson. When the *Welch Daily News* or the *Bluefield Daily Telegraph* arrived every day, the first thing all the adults did was to check the obituaries. Everyone came out to view the body, and it was important to show up on time—not too early and not too late. A lot of socializing took place, and it was good to be seen. The usual remarks could be heard. "Mrs. Tuscano had a good turn out." "Doesn't she look natural?" "She kept a nice house." If the weather was a problem, we said, "It is a shame it snowed or else more people would have shown up."

Prayer was important in the coalfields. Every day before school began, before any sporting event, before any patriotic event, or prior to any civic meeting, prayer was the norm and not questioned. Saying the Pledge of Allegiance and standing for the National Anthem were a part of what was right and good about America. Everyone was always proud and respectful. Never in a million years would a single Northfork citizen—young or old, native or foreign born—even consider not standing, hand over heart, for the Pledge, or not know every word to "My Country 'Tis of Thee" or "The Star-Spangled Banner."

CHAPTER 9

Living Over Mr. Parsons' Barbershop

Heading out of Northfork on Rt. 52 going towards Bluefield, you were on your way to our house. After veering left off Rt. 52, passing the old Angelo store, and crossing the railroad tracks, you were in Elkridge. I am not exaggerating when I say on many days we would not see the sun until about ten o'clock. Why? The fog would lie on the tops of the mountains and filter down slowly to the hollers. And because the sun moved behind those tall, high mountains by five o'clock, we never saw a sunset growing up. No wonder we now love Hawaiian, Memphis, and Carolina sunsets!

On our side of the road lived the Belchers: Ernie, his wife Charlene (always known as Chuck), and Wanda Lynn. They moved there while I was in grade school. Ernie, a coal miner, was a good musician. He'd have guys over, and they would play a lot of music and have a big time. Chuck was a lot of fun, and really idolized her daughter, Wanda Lynn. Wanda was very, very smart, and I looked up to her to steer me right when I went to junior high and then through high school. They always bought cars from Daddy.

On the right was a long row of brick houses, some several stories, and some one story. Some were built by Pete Capadini, and some by other builders. Old pictures show that the location of those brick houses was the site of the original coke ovens for the Elkridge Coal Company, hence, the name Elkridge. The coal companies used the coke ovens to create coke, which was used to manufacture steel. I don't know if the brick to build those houses came from all those brick coke ovens when they were torn down, but many of the houses had the same bright-red brick. Many of those houses were purchased by Italians. When or where the Italians got the money to buy the houses is uncertain, but I bet it was through hard work from daylight to dark and saving every penny they earned.

The first house in the row of houses was ours. It was a three-story house, including the full basement, and was owned by Pete Capadini. For twenty years, Mom and Dad rented that house for eighty dollars a month, not wanting to buy until they could pay cash. A mortgage was out of the question. This may have had something to do with the Great Depression and having ready cash to live on. Living in the Million Dollar Coalfields, everyone heated with coal—but not us. We had oil heat with steam radiators. Once a year the big oil truck from the Esso Bulk Plant would come and fill our oil tank with 250 gallons of heating oil. Since the house sat at the height of the coke ovens that had been carved out of the mountains, we had nineteen steep steps leading up from the main road to the first level of the house. We originally had a small, side yard and a small yard around the house. The front yard grass had to be dug up and replaced with gravel because Mr. Parson's barbershop was built in underneath the foundation of the house, and the barbershop ceiling leaked due to moisture. Just imagine that! We had a gravel front yard! A side driveway was created in the early 1960s and a large, side yard added. While we never had fresh-cut flowers in our house, in the summer Mother had window boxes of petunias and potted plants of geraniums. It was always strange telling people we lived in a big, brick house over the barbershop on the road to Crumpler hollow and try to make it sound like it was a nice house in a nice suburb of Northfork. From the front porch, you could see all of Elkridge and its houses, a lot of roofs, and even the colored church where the stork left me to hatch. To the left was the railroad track and Rt. 52. To the right, was the road leading to Crumpler and more brick houses. Looking directly across the rooftops, the high Appalachian Mountains rose skyward. This was a sight we saw every single day, but we didn't appreciate it until much later.

We were one of the first to get a gas-powered lawn mower; most still had the push type with the big cutting blades. Also unique was our portable swimming pool, about three feet deep. It was round with a hard, blue, plastic base, and its sides were supported by a white, plastic fence. No such thing as a filter. We would fill it with the garden hose, let the water warm up, and swim around. The water was good for about a week. We would let the water out, Mother would scrub down the pool, and we would start all over again. Even Mother would lay out in the sun with us, all greased up with our baby oil and iodine concoction, and then cool off in the water. Mother let me invite friends and neighbors when it was about time for us to clean it again.

We had a long, concrete front porch—not wood like most other houses. Every year Mother would have the porch floor painted red. We had aluminum porch furniture with plastic strips woven like potholders, arranged around a round, marble-topped table. To add more color, Mother set three-foot-high clay urns that she painted yellow on each side of the front door. The Algoma Coal Company's processing plant just up the road and the cinders from the coal train engines caused us lots of front-porch aggravations. Years away from pollution control, that long porch had to be swept or rinsed off just about every day. If Mother didn't clean the porch often, you could see your footprints as you walked across it. The porch problem was a bane in Mother's existence. But we never even had a key to lock our front door, or any other doors, as I remember. Open windows and doors were no problem since safety wasn't an issue, just the coal dust and cinders.

Coming through the front door was the entry hall. To its left was the long, open living room, running the entire thirty feet of the house. An enormously open space, Mother arranged the furniture to create areas of living spaces. The "piano area" included various chairs and side tables, and was where Martha and I performed "our presentations" for company. The far back wall—painted a dark red—was the backdrop for our Admiral cabinet television, and before that our cabinet radio and two matching bookcases. Nearby were easy chairs and a couch, making this our "TV room." Along the side wall—the longest wall in the house—sat a fake, wooden fireplace with mantel and fireplace tools, all lit by electric logs. This area featured couches and upholstered chairs centered with a round coffee table that got my niece, Laura, in much trouble when she was three years old. A large bowl of fresh apples always sat there—never eaten, but always on display. Laura bit into each apple, turned each over, and hid her crime. However, her tiny teeth marks gave her away, and she too landed in Mother's hot water. A very large room indeed, Mother had created an attractive room under the most difficult situation. She herself could not have imagined how forward-thinking her home décor had been. These days all any homeowner wants is an open floor plan.

With two large windows facing front, our dining room sat to the right of the entry and was filled with 1930s Drexel dining room furniture. We ate in the dining room every Sunday and every holiday, but we don't remember ever eating breakfast or lunch there. These two meals were always in the kitchen, a mere few steps away. The kitchen had a double window over the sink and a large, glass-brick window, common in most Italian-built houses, which was near the back door. On a nearby wall, a yellow wall phone hung over a small desk where Mother did all her check writing.

Mother had her own kitchen cabinets installed, and painted each one turquoise to match up with a turquoise Frigidaire stove and refrigerator. The real plaster walls were yellow, and the turquoise appliances made for a very fashionable 1960s kitchen. Mother's other unique kitchen feature was a "bar, as she called it. She drew a sketch, and had Grant Blevins build the centerpiece. The "bar" sat in the middle of the room, about waist high, with a yellow, Formica top and stools around all four sides. Beneath the countertop were enclosed shelves for storage. The sliding doors on each long side hid pots, pans, and glass serving dishes. Painted turquoise to match the appliances, Mother's "bar" was used for the next sixty years, eventually ending up in her laundry room for storage. Who would even guess that Mother's 1960s "bar" is now called a kitchen island.

Our linoleum-tile flooring was multicolored. Whenever the kitchen tile was scrubbed and then waxed with Mother's Johnson's Glo-Coat, she would put down sheets of newspaper—either the *Welch Daily News* or the *Bluefield Daily Telegraph*—to make sure the clean floors stayed clean. When one side got dirty, she turned the papers over. When company came, up came the newspapers. The kitchen door opened up to a small back porch with a wooden, two-seater swing. The lowest level—the basement—had four rooms, all named according to their purpose. The first room we called the "sitting room" held old living room furniture, but no one really did any "sitting" there. The "freezer room" was home base for the big freezer chest that Dad kept stocked with meat, big tubs of ice cream, and popsicles treats for us girls. On the floor was a sheet of plywood that Martha used to practice her tap dancing. We never called the "freezer room" the "tap dancing room" though.

The third room was the "laundry room" with its laundry tub, wringer washing machine, and ironing board. Using a wringer machine took skill, good arm muscles, and common sense, but all I ever heard was, "Jenna Lou, don't get so close to the wringer rollers or your arms will get crushed," or "Don't get close to the iron. You'll get burned." Only adults such as Mother, the cleaning woman, or Remmie could ever do laundry. Around the corner was a "toilet room." It was also known as Dad's "library." The last room was the oil "furnace room." None of the basement was too appealing to us girls since it was cold and damp. It always had a lot of moisture, being almost three-fourths underground. Push would come to shove when we tried to ride our bikes or roller-skate from room to room—a tight squeeze that caused scraped knuckles or skinned knees.

Four bedrooms finished off the top floor. We all shared one bathroom, but we never seemed to have a problem with this. There were no such things as bathrooms for each bedroom. In fact, some folks still had outhouses. Martha and I shared a corner bedroom with twin beds and lots of windows. As kids, we would lie in bed and listen to the trains and coal cars shifting back and forth on the main railroad tracks. Survival in our room wasn't easy. With small closets by today's standards, our bedroom was never used for playing or entertaining. The concept of "sleepover" had not come into our world. Martha would write in her diary with the red border, and she even had a red key. She wrote with a fountain pen and green ink. Dedicated to writing every night, Martha continued this through college and beyond. Always locking her diary and hiding the key was absolutely necessary, since I would read each entry and tell Mother everything I read. Martha has kept all of her diaries, and she still has "Red Diary Number One."

The strangest sight outside our side window was above the highway and the colored school nearby. It was a slag dump, or slate dump as Mother called it. This high mountain of coal was created when coal refuge or slag was dumped from high on the mountaintop down the sloping hillside. By day, it looked like a black mountain with no vegetation at all. At night, you saw the burning coal deposits smothering and burning coal residue, giving off bright colors of red, blue, green, and yellow fires. Sometimes the colors made straight, vertical lines up and down the hillside and other times the colors had no patterns at all, depending upon how the coal was dumped and how it burned. Usually the air smelled of burning sulfur, and if the air pressure was high, everything smelled like rotten eggs. We never thought the smoking slag pile was dangerous, and we two always admired the beauty of the colors at night. Martha and I always had our own private fireworks out our bedroom window, so we were never too impressed with the annual Fourth of July fireworks at the Starland Drive-In Theatre each summer.

Chapter 10

Miss Gee-Net

The house we lived in the better part of our youth was always neat, clean, and a showplace. One of the reasons everything stayed clean and fresh was Mother and Mae. Mae was married to Henry and lived on Colored Hill in Algoma. Even though Henry worked in the mines, Mae was Mother's "cleaning woman." Now Mae had a lot of children, so many in fact they had nicknames like "knee baby," "thigh baby," and "hip baby." Seems like she was always "pragnat," as Mother pronounced it. I remember Mae sitting on the ledge of our bedroom window, three stories high, cleaning the outside windows even while "pragnat." This is one of the few times I remember our window being opened. They always stuck, and since we had coal dust from the Algoma mine coating everything every day, it wasn't worth the trouble. Here is a classic scene: while Mae sat backwards on the windowsill cleaning the top outside windows, Mother stood with one hand on her hip and a cigarette in the other hand, pointing with that cigarette and saying, "Mae, you missed that spot right up there." I guess Mother did try to be considerate, because she would tell me to stop talking to Mae so I didn't distract her while she was hanging out the windows.

Washday was always Monday; ironing was Tuesday's job. The rest of the week was for cleaning. Mae helped with the wash on Mondays. After washing the clothes in the wringer washer and hanging them out to dry on double clotheslines stretching the length of the yard, Mae would use an old Coke bottle with a "sprinkle" head on the top. No such thing as a steam iron, the clothes would be "sprinkled" down, rolled up, and ready for ironing on Tuesday. Mother sent Daddy's dress shirts to the Tri-District Cleaners, but items like tablecloths had to be starched in ARGO starch that boiled in a pot. If the starch mixture was too thick, the clothes could literally stand up by themselves, stiff as a board! Mae helped with spring cleaning, fall cleaning, washing the bedroom and dining room curtains, floors, and just about anything "Miss Gee-net," as Mae called her, needed.

Mae ate lunch on the back porch steps during the summer and on the indoor basement steps in the winter. In the summer, I would eat lunch with her. I'd ask a million questions like, "Did you like going to school"? She would tell me she went to the colored school and the girls were really bad. She said they would cut each other up with knives and fight a lot. Mae added that they got the old books the white kids quit using, and the school wasn't in the best of shape. We'd laugh a lot and be having a good time until Mother would call outside and say it was time to get back to work.

When I began driving, I always begged to drive Mae home. She usually walked. Hopefully Mae wasn't too scared of riding with me, but I think she appreciated the ride after working for "Miss Gee-net" all day. She'd say she hoped she'd see some of the colored folks she knew so they could recognize her in "Miss Gee-net's" new car. I'd drive really slow hoping some of her friends would see her. The last time I remember seeing Mae was when Remmie died. She came and helped out at the house with the visitors and food. Henry bought cars from Daddy.

Chapter 11

Romeo's Store

My favorite place in Elkridge was Romeo's store. The store was as much a part of my everyday life as my home. I either walked or rode past it no matter where I was going. When I was in junior high, I caught the school bus there along with Wanda Lynn, Shelia Gravely, and Joe Giardina. During the winter months, we would go into the store and keep warm. Mr. Romeo always kept it toasty. The little, Italian gentleman was always so cordial and really nice to everyone. Not very tall, Carmine Romeo wore wire-rimmed glasses, was very neat in appearance, and had light-olive skin just like Dad's. Mrs. Romeo was tall, had pretty, dark hair, was just as pleasant as Mr. Romeo, and often helped him in the store.

It took seventy-two steps to get from the back porch of my house to Romeo's front door. There was a double, wooden door, but only one was unlocked. A bell rang to announce your arrival. I can still see "Romeo" painted on the front window—and how it looked backward from the inside of the window—with its big, black, sweeping "R" trimmed in red and gold. I clearly remember each part of his store. I remember the smell of fresh meats, and the sounds my feet made on that wooden floor.

On the store's left side sat a very tall counter. The bottom of it was black—sort of art-deco style. I couldn't reach the top of the counter most of my life since I was too short. The Wise Potato Chip stand sat on the high counter, and behind the counter were the cash register, ice cream freezers, and wall shelves that held canned goods and cleaning products like Glass Wax or Pride Furniture Polish. Sitting next to the counter was a big display of Betsy Ross and Sunbeam bread, Hostess Cupcakes, rolls, and various other bread products. A candy counter was also there. I loved the Necco wafers, Mallo Cups, Reese's Cups, and candy cigarettes. Straight back was a second room where Mr. Romeo had a wooden table with two wooden benches. He would play cards with Bessie Somanski when he wasn't busy. Sometimes I had to wait until they finished a game to get waited on. On the right side were more shelves with canned goods, cereal, a big meat case, and a counter with scales. The counter had a big roll of butcher paper with a sharp blade attached, like today's Saran Wrap dispenser. In front of the meat cooler were fresh vegetables in baskets.

We bought everything on account, and paid at the end of the month for our purchases. I went to Romeo's every day. We always purchased six Cokes in a carton. I carried the glass empties down in a metal Coca-Cola carrier with a big, steel handle, and took the new Cokes back home in it. A typical grocery order would include four pork chops, a loaf of Sunbeam Bread, a can of peas, and a candy bar for me. I had to tell Mr. Romeo what Mom wanted, and he would get them for me, going from one side of the store to the other. Mother always said, "Tell Mr. Romeo I want four NICE pork chops." He would take out the rack of pork, grab his meat cleaver, chop each one—BANG—hold each one in his hand, and say, "Is this a nice-a porka chop?" I would shake my head yes, like I knew, and he would pull off a big piece of butcher paper, lay down the pork chops, and wrap them up. He was really efficient in getting the white twine around the package to tie it up. Mr. Romeo would then take a brown paper bag, write down each item, and write the price with a pencil he kept behind his ear. I would say, "Mother said to put this on our bill." He would say, "Tell your mother I gave her "a nice-a porka chop." Of course I would tell Mother what he said, and she would just roll her eyes.

Sometimes I would just drop by to talk and say hello, sorta loaf around, and check out the new candy. We didn't think many of our neighbors had a monthly account. Mother said some of the other neighbors didn't want to give their money to Mr. Romeo; I had no idea what that meant. I do know a few of them drove all the way to Bluefield, Virginia, on a regular basis to grocery shop because the state of Virginia had no sales tax on food. The Romeos lived upstairs over the store, and it was quite spacious since it ran the full length of the store. They had a big swing on their top back porch, and I remember quite often seeing their youngest daughter, Dedo, swinging and listening to the radio.

Frequently some of the men would hang out in front of Mr. Romeo's store, sitting on a bench and watching the traffic going up Crumpler holler. Bessie Somanski hung out too. She always wore blue jeans and a plaid shirt, her hair in braids, and kept her cigarettes in her breast pocket. She smoked like a man and crossed one leg over the top of the other, sorta sideways. I saw her in a skirt once; I think it was for a funeral. She would always say, "HeyJennaLouhowyadoing," all in one word. I bet if she drove a car, she would have bought a car from Daddy.

Mr. Romeo's oldest daughter, Patty, was beautiful. Our band director, Litz Armbrister, said she was one of the best head majorettes he ever had. She went to Concord College, married her high school sweetheart, and both became prominent teachers in the county. Her husband, Jennings Boyd, became the most successful basketball coach in the state of West Virginia, setting a national record with eight straight basketball championships in the 70s and 80s. But good customers that we were, Mr. Romeo never bought a car from Daddy.

Chapter 12

Around Elkridge

Leaving Romeo's store and going up the left side of the road, you came to a small house where some older, colored people lived. It was a little house, and you never saw them out. Across the street sat a vacant lot, and anyone visiting them parked there. One Easter Sunday, I saw a big Oldsmobile parked there. I saw a colored family get out of the Oldsmobile. All were dressed up, the little girls in frilly dresses and ribbons in their hair. The man was all decked out in a smart suit and hat, and the woman was in a sleek, black suit with high heels. It was hard to believe. I asked Daddy who they were and why they dressed so fancy for coloreds. Making no sense to me, he said the "NDoubleACP" dressed them up. Being a small child, I didn't know if the "NDoubleACP" was a club, a person, or a church. One of the neighbors said the man "ran numbers" in Keystone, so they had a lot of money. I had no idea what any of it meant or even why. Whoever they were, they never bought a car from Daddy.

Close by lived two colored women named Thelma and Millie. Their house was small and set right on the highway. Thelma was a schoolteacher at the colored school, and her sister, Millie, didn't work. Everyone waved and said hello to them. Thelma had a great smile, was tall, and had several gold teeth. Remmie became good friends with Millie and would go sit on the porch and talk to her; but Millie never came to our house. One day they moved because they built a new house on Northfork hill, on the way to Burke. I bet they had thirty steps up to that house. I think Daddy insinuated that the "NDoubleACP" helped build that house, but who knows. Thelma bought one car from Daddy.

The next house sat directly across from us, and belonged to the Parsons. Elsie Parsons could do anything: make a garden, cook just about anything, can garden goods, kill snakes, or do carpentry work. She had a great big laugh, and due to the location of her house, she could see all the comings and goings in the neighborhood. Coming back from Myrtle Beach one summer, Elsie met Mom at the car to tell us that Mom's brother, Junior, and his "wife," had come to stay at the house while we were gone. So we had a clue that all may not be right, and it WAS NOT! Those two cooked steaks, left a mess, and even took pennies from our penny bank.

Charlie, Elsie's husband, ran the barbershop located underneath our house, and was a quiet, refined man. Alvenia, their daughter, was one of our favorites. She was cordial, a good dancer, and as jovial as her mother. Alvenia had a very fashionable, purple, satin baseball jacket with her name on it. She was in an organization called Rainbow Girls, and Elsie was big in the Eastern Star. Elsie wore her evening gown a lot to meetings. I never understood what the Eastern Star was, but knew it was a good thing. Elsie bought new cars every couple of years, usually a Ford station wagon that had enough wood on it to fill a forest. As good of friends and neighbors as we were, they only bought Ford products from Elkhorn Motors in Keystone. One year Elsie drove up with an olive-green Edsel. The Edsel, Ford Motor Company's newest auto, looked to be a strange design and was not the usual car color with its drab army green. I thought it was the ugliest car I'd ever seen! Elsie didn't keep her Edsel for long. I'll bet she wished she had though, since years later that model and color became a valued treasure.

Chapter 13

The Giardina Boys

To the right of our house, a brick fence separated us from the Giardinas. Their washhouse was also up against our side yard. The washhouse had a flat roof where the boys would play, and Sarah Jane would lie out there in the sun. Sarah was a year younger than Martha, and was really pretty. I thought she was cool. Her mother, Nannie, always called her "Sarah Jane-a." She used to play records in her room, which faced our house. On warm days, you could hear Sarah playing, "Little Darlin'," "Stagger Lee," or "Walking to New Orleans," while hanging out with Bonnie Cornett and Judy Simplicio. She took business courses in high school, but I don't think she was allowed to date much.

I loved playing games with the two younger Giardina boys. Joe was two years younger, and Jimmy was four years younger than I was. It made no difference. We ran, we played ball, we played cowboys, we shot marbles, and we played Bennett's Funeral Home. Playing Bennett's Funeral Home meant we would run around the yard making siren sounds and pretending to load bodies into the back of an ambulance, just like their big brother Dennis would do working for Mr. Bennett, the funeral director. The Funeral Home Game could be rather complicated.

We had to decide who would be the "body," who would be the "loader," and who would be the "driver." Each one of us wanted to be the "driver." No matter which was which, we all had to make the loud, siren sounds. Sometimes we would be so loud with our sirens, neighbors would come out on their porches to see what was wrong. I would love the summers when Nannie would make us tomato sandwiches and Kool-Aid. She made the best Italian bread, and would give us loaves. She also fried up her bread dough to make the best doughnuts!

Her husband, Frank, was a coal miner, and I remember him working the 3-11 p.m. shift over at Black Wolf. A watchful dad, he'd get up in the morning, sit in his chair backwards leaning against the porch banisters, smoke cigarettes, and be our baseball umpire. Our ball was made of tape. We would ball up newspaper and put black tape around it to make the ball. It didn't go far, but far enough to get to the end of the sidewalk. Even though the yard was on a slant, our bases were out in the yard. Poor Nannie never had a full lawn of grass because we ran paths from base to base. If one of the boys hit the ball into the highway, we'd have to stop playing while someone watched us go get it, and then start over again. We would definitely stop playing and go hide when Floyd walked by. A local hobo, he would shuffle along the road with a burlap sack over his shoulder. Frank always said, "Hey Floyd, would you like to have a couple of mean kids?" Floyd wore bib overalls and an old, wool hat. His big, burlap sack always flapped open. We were horrified that Floyd would grab us up, put us in that burlap sack, and throw us in the creek. Frank would take a draw of his cigarette and just laugh. Our other fear was when we heard the gypsies were in the area. If we misbehaved, we believed Frank would get them to take us away. Nannie also had trouble keeping her storm door clean—too many handprints and fingerprints from those boys.

One thing about the Giardina boys: being energetic and very competitive, they always ran everywhere. I never saw either of them walk. They would run to Romeo's store, they would run down the back alley to the creek, and Jimmy always tried to catch Joe running as fast as he could. The boys were somewhat shy and somewhat afraid of Mother. That meant Mother had a hard time communicating with Joe and Jimmy. I didn't. One hot, summer afternoon, the boys and I were playing Cowboys and Indians in our backyard. Mother came out and asked if we wanted a Popsicle. I answered, but the boys did not. Mother looked at me and said, "Do the boys want a Popsicle?" I looked at each of them and said, "Yes." Mother said, "What flavor do you want, cherry or grape?" I said, "Cherry." They didn't answer. Mother looked again to me and I said after looking at them, "Joe wants grape, Jimmy wants cherry." And so in any conversation around my mother, I was the interpreter.

Every time I ran next door to play with the Giardina boys, Mother never missed a chance to warn me, "Jenna Lou, if you don't slow down running with those boys, you're going to fall and break every bone in your body." So one time I ran, fell, and broke my arm. Off to the Stevens Clinic Hospital we went for x-rays and a cast, causing Mother to postpone our yearly trip to Washington, PA and a visit with Aunt Gladys and Uncle Bill. In all of Mother's concern also came, "I told you to slow down."

Nannie, like many Italian ladies, spoke both English and Italian very well. I wish I had learned some Italian from her. In 1960, the New York Yankees were playing the Pittsburgh Pirates in the World Series. We had a color TV; the Giardinas hadn't gotten a color set yet, so Mother actually let Joe come over one afternoon to watch one of the games. I think that was the only time he was in the house. He enjoyed the game, and I think Mother even gave him a Coke.

Even though we lived in the mountains, we didn't have a lot of snakes or any mice thanks to the Giardinas' cats. We didn't appreciate it at the time, but those cats walking on the fences kept the snakes and mice away. Those cats had a lot of gangster names, but Baby Face Nelson was my favorite cat of the bunch. When I was in high school—after Sarah left for Washington, DC—Nannie and I talked a lot, and she was just the best. She'd say, "Jenna Lou, you are so silly." Frank was one of my favorites, but a man of few words. He was always kind to me and laughed at my stupid jokes. They didn't go on many vacations, but in the 1960s they did go to the ocean. When Frank came back, he told me in great detail how he loved sitting in a beach chair watching the waves "come in" and "go out." While they were wonderful neighbors, the Giardinas always bought Chevrolets from Carroll's.

Chapter 14

More Elkridge Favorites

On up the road lived the Gravely family. Shelia was one of my good friends; Martha was in the same class as Shelia's sister Billie. I loved Mrs. Gravely. She was the most realistic person in Elkridge, said what she thought, and did what she wanted without worrying about what others thought. Shelia had some good pajama parties, and Mrs. Gravely helped it happen. The Gravelys bought cars from Daddy.

The Simplicios lived at the end of Elkridge. Their house was made of yellow brick, which was very unusual. They had a store underneath their house and had ten children. While Mr. Simplicio worked as a coal miner, the older children helped Mrs. Simplicio in the store. For many Northfork girls, the older Simplicio girls became role models as they went to Washington, DC, after graduation, getting good government jobs. Nancy was Martha's best friend, and I loved it when all the Simplicio girls would return home on the holidays with all their adventure stories about DC and wearing their "city" high heels. (Mother could never figure out how some of those girls from Landgraff and Maybeury could go to Washington, DC, as a clerk typist in August and come home with mink coats at Christmastime!) Mrs. Simplicio canned delicious green peppers in tomato sauce, and we loved getting them. One son, Luke, was really good looking. He had a charming personality—even as a young boy—and was a great dancer. I can't name one girl who didn't have a crush on him, especially me. Some of the Simplicio children bought cars from Daddy.

Another favorite Elkridge family was the Morellos. All were musical, smart, and had engaging personalities. Mary, the mother, held rosary for us kids and had a very positive outlook on life. I can still see Joe, Joanne, and Sammy entertaining at local events—Joe with his accordion, and the others singing beautifully. At times their mom and dad would accompany them too. Before they purchased a television, they would come by some Saturday nights and watch Big-Time Wrestling. As I remember, the Morellos did not buy cars from Daddy.

I couldn't complete the Elkridge favorites without the Arenas. This family of four lived on the other side of the Giardinas. Very religious, Sue Arena was an outstanding cook of Italian cuisine. In fact, she taught Mother how to make spaghetti sauce. We could never figure out if Sue or Nannie made the best Italian bread, because both were wonderful. To this day, when I smell freshly baked bread, it always calls up Sue and Nannie's breads. The priest regularly visited and enjoyed Sue's cooking as well. All of us kids knew not to scream and yell when playing while the priest was there visiting Sue. Martha's very best friend most of her school life was Joe, the Arena's oldest. From the fourth grade through the twelfth grade, those two were friends in school and out. They shared classes, school projects, and high school life. Joe excelled in math, in all levels from Algebra I to Trig and beyond. Martha excelled in the language area. They traded skills, and both graduated at the top of their class. Sue was my confirmation sponsor and liked to talk to me about religion, being a good girl, and life in general. The Arenas bought Oldsmobiles from Carroll's. Sixty years later their house became a bed-and-breakfast stop on the popular McDowell County ATV trail.

Chapter 15

Sign of the Times

In the 1950s, Elkridge and the other little towns around did not have garbage service, nor was there a town dump for any garbage drop-offs. Everyone either burned their trash in a "burn barrel" or threw their garbage in the creek. Martha had one job, and that was the creek garbage. Every day Martha would carry at least one bag of garbage in the large, brown grocery bags—plastic bags not yet invented—down the nineteen steep steps, across the road, and down the back alley to Elkhorn Creek. During that process, Martha's worst nightmare was when the brown paper bag would leak, and the garbage would fall out of the bottom. Mother told her the same thing every day, "Be sure to throw the bag in the middle of the creek." Not only was that to ensure the bag didn't get caught up on the creek bank, but to be sure no one saw what was in our garbage. Sometimes I walked with her. When she stood on the wall along the creek bank and threw in the garbage, there would be lots of other bags bobbing down the creek. Between the garbage in the creek and the residue from the coal mines, the creek was totally black. Whenever I asked, "Why are our creeks black here and not black in Alaska?" The standard answer would be, "What do you want, clean creeks or people starving if the mines don't work?" Ironically, in the late 1960s I was chosen West Virginia Water Festival Queen, and strangely enough one of the proclamations I made included, "...to keep pure the mountain streams, rivers, and lakes from contamination and unsightly filth and liter...." Fortunately, reclamation of the slag dumps, filters for coal cinders, and cleaning up the creeks had begun, which proved within the next fifty years that coal mining and a clean environment can mix.

It's interesting that in the 1950s women were known by their titles and their marital status, such as "Mrs. Roy Keesee," not given names such as "Jesse Keesee." Joint checking accounts were listed as "Mr. and Mrs. Roy Keesee." Newspaper articles referred to a married woman by her husband's name, such as "Mrs. Floyd Giampocaro was inducted into the Junior Women's Club," not "Ann Giampocaro." Single women or old maids were identified as "Miss Julia Crown." Prefixes were always used. An old maid was defined as a woman who was not married by age twenty-one. Thank goodness the times slowly began to change in the early 1960s. Men did not use vulgar language around women, and no lady swore in public. Funny though, I heard many jokes about bad women drivers. Those were our pre-blonde jokes. Those jokes made me madder than the ones about a Wop or a Tally. Since there were no nail shops, the only time some lady got a manicure was at the beauty shop—now known by the fancy name of hair salon—and I never knew anyone who had a pedicure. Tattoos were for servicemen, motorcycle-gang members, or thugs. The only women who got tattoos were in the side show at the carnival.

Northfork did have one trendsetter, Reba Norris Carroll. Her husband owned the Chevrolet/Oldsmobile/Cadillac dealership, and she managed the office. After her husband died, Mrs. Carroll became the first lady Chevrolet dealer in the United States. She was a civic leader, went to the Democratic National Convention representing West

Virginia, was a vocalist in the choir, smoked a lot, wore the best clothes, had the biggest house, and kept her pulse on everything happening in Northfork. She was sorta the Leona Helmsley of Northfork, but very nice and very charitable. It was said that Mrs. Carroll really ran the Baptist Church since she was the biggest money contributor. During the early years when Daddy worked for the Carrolls, Mrs. Carroll was always very good to Martha and me. After Daddy got his Pontiac dealership, she was his biggest competitor.

Chapter 16

The Wonderful Word of Television

Big news in 1955! We became members of the Elkridge Television Club, which meant we got a television and cable service. Since we were in the hollers of the mountains, Fred Little and his cable company—a new concept—installed his antenna on top of the mountain and then ran a line to each house.

Some folks did not choose to get hooked up to Mr. Little's cable, so they sat a portable antenna, called "rabbit ears," on top of their TV and wiggled the antenna wires to get a clearer reception. Our Admiral TV sat in a big, wooden cabinet, matching the other living room furniture. Some others might have had a tabletop model. Now TV replaced the radio as the main source of home entertainment. We watched the new television, even when it wasn't on! There were no round-the-clock broadcasts, just six o'clock in the morning to midnight. The first image on the screen was a test pattern. This allowed the viewers to adjust their sets for black or white brightness. Before long, we could choose the networks—NBC, ABC, or CBS—and each network had their local stations. We would get excited when we heard, "Live from New York the

National Broadcasting Company is on the air," and then we would hear the NBC chime. The test pattern was on after all the shows went off too.

The *Today Show* with Dave Garroway was a hit in the house. One year when Daddy went to the World Series in New York City, we spotted him in the crowd around the window, not unlike the crowds outside the early morning TV shows today. I knew when all the programs came on, knew all the commercials, and who starred in every show. At night Daddy would say to me, "Hey, Cat Bird, what is on TV tonight?" I would recite what was on all three channels.

Remmie loved to watch the soap operas, fifteen-minute-long programs. Her favorite, *Search for Tomorrow*, was sponsored by Duz or Tide, and sometimes by Joy. We loved the cigarette commercials. The Old Gold commercial had dancing girls wearing costumes that looked just like a pack of regular cigarettes, a filtered pack of cigarettes, and a pack of matches. All you saw of the girls were their legs and their high heels. I always wanted to be the pack of matches when I grew up. I knew all their dance steps. We also liked the Philip Morris commercials on *I Love Lucy* that featured Johnny, a small person dressed up like a page in a hotel saying, "Call for Philip Morr-rris."

We would watch the evening news with John Cameron Swayze, wearing his Timex watch and saying the following slogan, "It takes a licking and keeps on ticking." On Saturday, Martha and I would watch the *Sealtest Circus* at noon and eat tomato soup and peanut butter sandwiches in front of the TV. When TV dinners became big, Mother loved it. She also purchased TV trays and let us eat in front of the TV on special occasions; however, we mostly ate meals in the kitchen on a regular basis. We liked quiz shows like *You Bet Your Life*, with Groucho Marx, *I've Got a Secret*, or *What's My Line*. Daddy would watch *Meet the Press* on Sundays after all the church shows. He especially liked watching the Macy's Thanksgiving Day and Rose Bowl parades.

As a kid, the *Howdy Doody Show* was my very favorite, along with *Winky Dink*. Howdy was on every weekday at five o'clock, but Winky was only on Saturday before *Sky King*. For *Winky Dink*, we had this special adhesive film that was applied to the TV screen. Purchased at G. C. Murphy's, the film came with special pens you could use to help Winky out of situations. The film went on and came off easily from the TV screen. Before there was *Captain Kangaroo*, there was *Ding Dong School* with Miss Frances. While it was for the kindergarten set, I would still watch, especially when Miss Frances would tell the children to go get their mothers so she could give them an important message at the end of the show.

Of course, *American Bandstand* became an afternoon favorite from the mid-50s through high school for Martha and me. I even still have my Frani Giordano Fan Club Membership Card since she was my favorite dancer. Sunday night in the 50s was *Candid Camera* night; and later in the 60s, *Bonanza* in living color. We purchased a color TV as soon as they were for sale at K&K Television in Northfork.

The Sunday-night staple, though, was the *Ed Sullivan Show*. Martha remembers the premiere of Elvis Presley on Ed's show. All the teenagers knew Elvis Presley would be on, and Martha wasn't going to miss it. Remmie was watching it with her, and Remmie called Mother into the living room and said, "Jenny, look at this disgraceful, white trash Martha Frances is watching!" Martha and I got a big laugh when we went through Graceland not too long ago, thinking about how things certainly have changed. Other big favorites were *77 Sunset Strip*, *Your Hit Parade*, *The Tonight Show*, *Father Knows Best*, *Dragnet*, *I Led Three Lives*, and *Gunsmoke*.

I never could figure out how everything always ended so nicely and all the problems were solved in shows like *Ozzie and Harriett* or *Leave it to Beaver*. Mother and Daddy did not act like the Cleavers. Their personalities mixed like oil and water, so their problem-solving tools mainly consisted of total disagreements. When being playful, Daddy would pick Mother up and put her on top of the refrigerator—one that wasn't that tall. Unlike Mrs. Cleaver, Mother would say, "Hello-Pete, Luke, get me down."

Amos and Andy was very popular, and the only coloreds we ever saw on TV back then. We believed everything we saw on TV, in the movies, and in the newspaper. Remmie loved *Queen for a Day*, starring Jack Bailey. It came on at three o'clock weekdays and catered to the housewife. The announcer would say, "Would you like to be Queen for a Day?" The audience would scream YES, and so would Remmie and I. Then the show would begin. Several women would tell their sad story, and the audience would pick the winner—usually the one with the most heart-wrenching situation. The winner would wear a crown, a robe, hold a scepter, and then be awarded prizes, such as a new washing machine, living room furniture, and a case of furniture polish or ARGO starch—"every housewife's dream."

We didn't become couch potatoes because we were too busy with school, piano lessons, and playing outside. Mother did start us snacking at night while we watched our favorite shows. We'd eat chips, Jiffy Popcorn, Wise or Pringles potato chips, or fried donuts. The fried donuts came from a can in the freezer section of Krogers. After she popped open the can, she would fry them up.

Another big purchase was our hi-fi set. This had a matching, wood cabinet and was designed to load several records at a time, play a single 78 or 45 record, automatically drop that record, and begin another. We collected a lot of albums, and usually played the hi-fi during and after supper. The hi-fi now seems like a primitive device compared to today's five-player CD or iPod.

Chapter 17

We Make the News

Mother was active in local civic groups including the Women's Club, was President of the PTA, and played on the women's basketball team. Seems like Mother and Daddy were in the local papers a lot, usually the *Welch Daily News*, the *Bluefield Daily Telegraph*, or the *Sunset News*. One article in the early 1950s said, "Carroll Motors Manager, Luke Gianato, Avid Sports Fan." He was featured along with a photo of him in a big bow tie. The article quoted him as saying he "has no time for hobbies. If he had one, it would probably be selling cars." It was a great PR piece for Carrolls, and also mentioned Dad's love of all sports and of his World Series trips. It described his distinguished war record, his being past commander of the VFW, his being on the board of directors of the Kimball Rotary, and of his past businesses in the clothing and restaurant business. In 1953, Mother was featured in an article entitled, "Women of Northfork." Pictured in the paper with other ladies, the women were cited for their civic contributions, Home Room Mothers' activities, and helping to get new grade school playground equipment.

Martha and I even got into the newspapers for piano recitals and church choir activities. Martha was featured as the Spring Carnival Queen at the junior high and was featured regularly for academic successes. One piano recital Martha played a piano piece, and I did a ballerina dance. I had not had lessons, and made it up as I went along. Remmie made my little, white tutu with a fluffy skirt, and I borrowed toe shoes from another little girl. I had never even been in toe shoes before I danced at the recital. Everyone said it was good, and we even had a professional photo taken.

After Dad went into business for himself, there were lots of newspaper and radio ads for his business in Northfork, and then for both of the businesses when he opened his dealership in Welch. He always had newspaper specials on occasions like April Fools' Day, the kickoff of the new football season, and Veterans Day. Some of the ads even featured the old dog, Blue, that hung around the garage. At Powhatan, Daddy had a huge billboard in the big curve of the road, right past the Powhatan Tavern, with his picture and the merits of buying from Gianato. We always loved that sign.

Chapter 18

Bennett Blue Book to Pizza Pie

We acknowledged birthdays at home. Presents were not a big deal, but having a birthday cake with a few presents was the norm. One year I did get a red fire truck. I could sit in it, push the pedals like a tricycle, and it would go. I could pull a string that went from my steering wheel to a little bell on the hood. That was my siren. It had two ladders I could take off and climb on. I rode it up and down the short sidewalk by my house. I never figured why I got a fire truck since it wasn't girly-girly, but I liked it.

We had a lot of catalogs that we ordered from, especially at Christmas. While we did get the Sears and JCPenney catalogs, I loved the Bennett Blue Book. It came with a hard, glossy, blue cover, and Mother said businesspeople got it. I loved to look at the jewelry—especially the diamond rings, always dreaming of what my engagement ring would look like.

Daily routines followed a pattern. We ate three good meals a day—or at least they were prepared for us to eat. Daddy or Remmie fixed breakfast. In the early years, we mainly took our lunch to school, but sometimes we ate in the cafeteria. I took my Hopalong Cassidy lunch box, and Martha took a paper lunch bag. By that time, the older kids quit using a lunch box.

For the evening meal—which we called supper—Mother always set the table nicely, and we had to use our napkins. A typical meal was stuffed peppers, mashed potatoes, and peas. We would also have a dessert, often pudding or pie. We always said the following blessing: "Lord we thank thee for what we are about to receive. Lead us and guide us throughout the day. Amen." Sometimes Remmie would add in, "Brother Ben, shot a rooster and killed a hen," and we would all laugh. We ate supper around six o'clock or whenever Daddy got home. He would sell a car at any time—including Sunday, Christmas, and Halloween—and our world would wait for the most part. We also learned to wait in the car a lot while he ran into the dealership for a "few minutes." Every Sunday we had roast beef with carrots, potatoes, and onions. The other standard was fried chicken, green beans, and potato salad. Easter had deviled eggs added; Christmas and Thanksgiving added turkey, dressing, and gravy. Remmie often baked her famous chocolate cake, Daddy's favorite. The recipe we can never replicate came from Mother's *Kimball PTA Cookbook*. Remmie put the recipe to memory, and Mother lost the cookbook. Even today, we remember this two-layer, chocolate delight with the creamy, chocolate icing on top.

On Wednesdays, Daddy had Kiwanis. Mother, Martha, and I would go to the Curb-In on the lower end of town. Owned by Louie Pannell, the Curb-In specialized in great hamburgers, french fries, and hot dogs. Instead of eating in our cars on Wednesdays, we went into the dining room to eat spaghetti and meat sauce cooked to perfection. Sometimes we would see Leilia Wallace and her kids, Carole and Gary. He always played Patti Page's hit, "How Much Is That Doggie in the Window," on the jukebox. On Sundays in the summer, Daddy grilled hamburgers and hot dogs. Otherwise, Daddy would get takeout on Sunday night or sometimes make us pancakes.

About four times a year—for no particular reason or event—Mother would get the urge to make fudge. One day out of the blue she would declare she was making fudge. Martha and I would get really excited to eat the best fudge in the world! She started by putting butter, sugar, cocoa, and some other ingredients together. At some point she would add a big spoon of peanut butter, and stir and stir with her giant spoon. Near the end, Mother would take a bit of the fudge mixture and drop it into a measuring cup of water. If the mixture formed a ball, the fudge was ready to place on the plate. That's when the fun would begin. I would get to lick the spoon, and Martha got to scrape the pan. We were very thorough, and there would be nothing left on either one. When we both went to college, Mother would sometimes send us a tin can full of fudge. What a treat! Unfortunately we did not get this recipe either, and have found very few times in our life when we have tasted a duplicate of that fudge.

Historical family moments always make an impression on your brain. Surprising us one day, Daddy stopped by this old joint in Huntington, West Virginia. He went in, and after what seemed like a century later, he came out with a big, square box with something that he called "pizza pie." It smelled funny at first, and I yelled, "Daddy, it smells like vomit!" Daddy said, gritting his teeth and yelling back, "Eat it, you'll like it!" We were initiated. Within a couple of years, Chef Boyardee came out with boxed pizza, and everyone made it. There were no pizza shops and no such thing as McDonald's in McDowell County. We ate hamburgers, maybe a hot dog, and sometimes a BBQ with coleslaw at local mom-and-pop joints.

Chapter 19

High as Georgie Pine

Mother and Daddy's best friends were Tony and Elizabeth Larkin. Both were like an aunt and uncle to us. We grew up playing with their sons, Tony Mack and Dickie. We were together many Sundays and holidays, particularly on late Christmas afternoons, exchanging presents and having lots of fun. Elizabeth was always talking about someone being as high as Georgie Pine. They did have a friend in Vermont named George Branch, so I got him confused with Georgie Pine. It was years before I realized Georgie Pine was not a person but a reference to someone being drunk, thus "as high as a Georgia pine." Uncle Tony always used to "catch my nose" with his thumb and call me a "Little Tally." The relatives would kid me that I was part "Tally" and part "Sager." I guess "Sager" meant not Italian, but I never thought anything negative about the nickname because they would just laugh and laugh. I could never figure out if my left side was "Tally" and the right side "Sager" or if it was the reverse.

Adults in our lives enjoyed some alcohol on holidays and a drink in the evening hours as we got older. We always had beer in the refrigerator. Sometimes Tony and Elizabeth played cards with Mother and

Daddy and had drinks. So it was no big deal about having a drink in our house. Many of my friends' parents were closet drinkers or strictly forbade it. Growing up, I never even saw my parents tipsy. So when I got to college, having a rum and Coke was just not taboo.

However, most everyone sure smoked those Lucky Strikes, Kents, and Kools. We had cigarette boxes and cigarette lighters all over the house. According to Mother, poor people used matches. It was most fashionable for the ladies to have a really nice cigarette case and matching lighter, usually attached by a chain. Smoking was not banned from any place. Therefore, Mother, like everyone else, smoked in grocery stores, department stores, ladies' shops, drugstores, doctors' offices, restaurants, sporting events, automobiles, and airplanes—anywhere at any time. She was cool though. She had a very small, metal box in her purse with a cloisonné picture of a cigarette. She called it her silent butler. She could smoke a cigarette, rub the fire out in the box, and then put the cigarette butt in the box, close it, and put it back in her purse. She said ladies didn't put out their cigarette on the streets—another of Mother's strict social rules. Everyone who I thought was interesting smoked cigarettes. This included aunts, uncles, Mother, Daddy, family friends, clergy, teachers, movie stars, shopkeepers, and all coal miners. Smoking became a rite of passage. You could always hear Daddy's army phrase around the house or the dealership, "Smoke 'em if you got 'em." Martha started when she went to college, clearing the path for me. Years later we all laughed when we figured out that at any one time in our house during a twenty-four hour period, someone was smoking. I would fall in love with a guy if he knew how to hold and smoke a cigarette the "right" way.

Our parents did not use foul language in front of us girls. What would people think? Daddy would cuss, saying damn and hell, but if Mother said "She-it" or "Hell-o Pete," it was a big deal. I never even heard the "F" word." African-Americans were called colored or "Tutsone" by the

Italians. Negro was too formal. Per Mother, the "N" word was only used by white trash. Mother forbade the use of that word in our house, not because she was racially sensitive or politically correct but because white trash used it. I really knew no one who was racially sensitive. It was different times.

Chapter 20

Poor People Drink Water

It seemed to me the only people who I saw drink water were poor. The only time I remember drinking any amount of water was at the school water fountain. There was no bottled water, and we didn't put glasses of water on the table at any meals. Everyone I knew drank coffee, milk, pop, or even Kool-Aid. We never had brewed coffee; instead we drank Nescafe instant coffee. For some reason, Mother hated to perk coffee. I never drank "real" coffee until I went to college. The only time we drank iced tea was vacation time at Myrtle Beach, and I never remember anyone drinking hot tea. We never drank wine. The only reference to wine was when Mother would call someone a "wino."

Before welfare was in place, we used to get a lot of beggars coming to the back door—never the front door. One summer day a beggar man knocked on the back screen door and asked for a "drink of water." I told Mother his request. Mother said, while puffing on her cigarette, "Give him a can of peas." I did wonder if he was so poor, how he would open the can of peas, and where he would cook the can of peas. Mother would just blow off a question like that by rolling her eyes at me.

Chapter 21

The Games Children Play

"One potato, two potatoes, three potatoes, four," was the start of us kids choosing sides to play our team games. "O-U-T, you're out" finished up the choosing chant, and football, baseball, tag, or hide-and-seek could begin. With no such things as playdates, organized children's sports, or school field trips, we created our own games and pastimes. Jump rope, card games, dolls, paper dolls, balls, bike riding, and sidewalk games were our games of choice. When I wasn't bugging someone to play cards with me, we girls would play "paper dolls," cutting out our paper doll clothes, and then attaching the clothes to each doll with a little tab. Martha was good at cutting, but I tended to cut off some of the tabs, making a mess and having the clothes fall off the dolls.

Hopscotch was challenging. We didn't have chalk. In fact, the only chalk we knew of was school chalk, so we had to draw our hopscotch grid with a rock. First we had to find the kind of rock that would a make a line on the concrete. After looking and looking, we would draw the grid and then play. We spent more time making the grid and finding a flat rock to pitch on the grid than we did actually "hopscotching."

Sometimes Mother would come out and play hopscotch with us. She was really good.

Throwing the ball against the house was a big pastime, and so was jumping rope. We would jump with a small rope by ourselves. Then we would tie two ropes together, tie one end to the fence, and then one of us would turn the rope for the other. Martha got the short end of that deal since I wasn't tall enough to turn the rope for her height. In the summer, we would pick pokeberries from the side hill, sneak them under the long front porch, and make ink. We would be covered with berry juice and once again get in hot water. I never remember anyone using the ink for writing.

There was nothing better than getting a new coloring book and new Crayola crayons. We colored and colored. Those original crayons required skill in staying inside the lines. Our crayon sharpener just didn't do a good job keeping our crayon tips sharp, not anything like the Crayola DigiTools kids these days use with their electronic tablets. Martha's friends traded a lot of funny books, but I just looked at the pictures. Martha was a big reader. She read all the Nancy Drew and Hardy Boys books and even the *Welch Daily News*. I thought reading was boring, but I did finally get into comic books. I liked dressing up in Mother's good clothes and fur piece, pretending I was a movie star like Doris Day.

Around the first week of June, just before dark, the lightning bugs came into season. We would get an old jar, have Mother punch holes in the top with her big butcher knife, and we would run around the yard catching away. We would put the lightning bugs in the jar, screw the cap on, and watch them light up as it got darker and darker. Martha showed me how to take the "light" off the bug and make a ring for my hand. When she outgrew catching the lightning bugs, I would catch them with Joe and Jimmy.

Of course we learned to hula hoop and play board games like Sorry or Monopoly. We even had a Beat the Clock game, based on the popular TV show. Popular group games were Drop the Handkerchief, Red Rover, and Mother May I. One time Martha and I were given a chemistry set. We had to use it in the damp basement. Martha did all the experiments since I didn't like to read directions. I think all the powders got damp because of the basement's climate. All the experiments seemed to fizzle out, so we lost interest.

Both Martha and I had cameras growing up. Martha started with a Brownie. Mine was more sophisticated and it had flashcubes! We took a lot of photos. We had them developed at the drugstore or sent them to Best Photo Company in Parkersburg, West Virginia. It would take at least a week to get the pictures back. We would literally go to the post office twice a day, waiting on the two mail sorts, to see if our photos arrived. It was so much fun to finally see the pictures. There was no instant gratification like today. We learned it is good to be patient and wait for good things to happen, even when you don't want to wait.

Life is funny in many ways. Decades later, Martha taught Photography to junior high kids, setting up a darkroom, developing film, printing photos, and teaching camera techniques. These classes through the years provided all the black-and-white photos for their school newspaper and yearbook. Maybe the love of photography for her started with that Brownie camera back when we were kids!

Chapter 22

Tiger Suit Tradition

Every Halloween we dressed up for trick or treat. In the fourth grade, Martha got a tiger suit. It was handed down to me. I wore the tiger suit from the time it was too big until I grew out of it, which had to have been at least five years.

This tiger costume with orange and black stripes was unique and special. Daddy purchased the costume on one of his October trips to see the New York Yankees in the World Series. We kept the Macy's bag it came in for years, saving it just to impress one of our friends, but the Macy's bag fell apart before anyone ever saw it. That's what we got for trying to be so snooty!

The costume itself came in four pieces. The first was a one-piece suit with arms, legs, and a long, stuffed, tiger tail. A hat with ears, which tied under the chin, was the second piece. Next came booties that slipped over the shoes. Lastly, there was a plastic, full-face, tiger mask. All but the mask was made of a lightweight cotton material.

The costume was awesome, and we girls never knew anyone who had a Halloween costume from Macy's. Martha wore the costume in its entirety for three years of trick-or-treating. Of course by year two, everyone knew the tiger's true identity.

The booties fell by the wayside first; the next year, the plastic mask cracked. Even though I could not breathe through the mask, I wore it anyway. I never thought to use mascara to put on whiskers and decorate my face like a tiger. But using that mask prepared me for years of wearing uncomfortable high heels just for looks! By the time I grew enough to wear the costume, all that was left was the body of the costume and the cracked mask—and I had to carry the tail because it lost its stuffing and had gone limp.

Mother always gave me a bar of soap to use on windows of those who did not answer their door. Of course, everyone around our house answered the door and gave us candy. I did soap up the windows of the open storefront below our house. The soap stayed for months, until the rain and snow eventually cleaned them off.

Chapter 23

Best Gnocchi in the World

As children, most of our contact with Daddy's family was during the holidays—Christmas, Easter, Fourth of July, and family birthdays. Those family members lived in Kimball, about six miles from Northfork. Rosie, otherwise known as Nonna, was Daddy's stepmother. A religious lady, Nonna was the family's matriarch, raising five young children after her husband— our grandfather—died, and at the same time operating the family grocery store.

Nonna's had a natural gift for hospitality, providing meals through the years for the local priests and anyone else who needed food. Nonna held her family close. Her love and caring carried over to the grandchildren, and later to the great-grandchildren. It was always a big thrill for the younger ones to measure their heights, comparing it to the four-and-a-half-foot Nonna. Being even an inch taller than her, made the youngsters feel grown-up. At any time, little ones could get hugs, kisses, and attention from Nonna.

Nonna lived over the store, but dinner in the big kitchen in back of the store was the big event, especially at Christmas. Relatives and friends from near and far always wanted to be with the Kimball family for the best food and company. Nonna, the aunts, and sometimes the uncles planned for days, cooking up the best gnocchi and spaghetti, along with all the traditional American Christmas foods. Everyone had lots of fun with all the uncles, aunts, and cousins. It was a big day, especially for us girls.

One after-dinner ritual found everyone piling into the kitchen to watch Nonna open her Christmas gifts. It took a while, but everybody had lots of fun, commenting on what gift she got and questioning which ones she would use. The consensus was "Not many!" Nonna always said most of her gifts would go into her cedar chest to be saved for later.

Uncle Mike ran the grocery store with Nonna and would close the store for the entire day on those special holidays. However on Christmas Day, for instance, some poor soul would always need bread or milk. Of course, they would get it from one of my uncles with a knock on the side door. For Christmas, Nonna gave each family an applesauce cake—the best-ever applesauce cake. Even after we grew up, Nonna gave the adults and the grandchildren with families an applesauce cake. One year, somehow Martha's applesauce cake was left in her car trunk. It stayed there frozen all winter. Don, her husband, said the cake was so solid he could have used it as a spare tire!

Any holiday at the store was always special. Years when all "The Family" was there, tables would be set up in the store for the overflow crowd. Laughing, talking, talking, and stories reigned supreme. There isn't a Gianato today who doesn't talk with their hands, hug, and love as Nonna did.

Our Kimball relatives were our Italian family, all seeming to gravitate toward Daddy. They asked his advice, and seemed to hold him in the highest esteem. Uncle Mike's wife, Lora Mae, was one of my role models. As a kid, I would play "Lora Mae" as I pretended to be working at the business offices of the Stevens Clinic Hospital, just as Lora Mae had very successfully done. Aunt Marie moved to Charleston, holding the office supervisory position at the West Virginia Supreme Court, and married Nick, an industrial engineer. Uncle Jimmy, a purchasing agent for the largest coal company, had a beautiful wife named Mary, who was an accomplished nurse. Uncle Johnny was in insurance and mining. His wife, Beulah, and Mother were the only two women we ever knew who smoked in Nonna's kitchen. As with many Italian families, most nephews were named in some variation of Luke, John, Mike, or Jim—after each of the brothers.

As young girls, Martha and I loved going to the store any time of the year. Uncle Mike would say, "Get a paper bag and pick out all the candy you want." That tradition continued in later years with my daughter, Jennifer, and Martha's daughter, Laura. As adults, we grew even closer to Nonna and the rest of the family. Before my second husband, Jim, and I were married, I took him to Kimball to meet the family. I was a little nervous since I wasn't sure what Nonna would think. After we walked in the door and introductions were made, Nonna quickly pulled me aside. Then I was really nervous. She said with a smile on her face, "When Jim walked through that door, I had to do a double take. Still a little nervous, I asked, "Why?" Nonna said, "He looks just like your granddaddy!" From that point on, they talked and talked. I believe she fell in love all over again, just like me. (She did make us promise her we would go through the annulment process from our first marriages so we could be married in the Catholic Church. We did.) When I went home and told Mother that story, she just rolled her eyes.

Chapter 24

Our Sunday Adventures

When we were little girls, we took lots of Sunday drives as a family. My special place in the car was standing on the edge of the backseat. I leaned on the back of Daddy's seat on my elbows, watching him drive. Seat belts didn't exist. Of course, this position would give Daddy a major headache since I was always talking or singing directly into his right ear. Martha sat behind Mother, and we would go to Beckley on the new turnpike—the "modern, three-lane highway,"—and eat at the Glass House. Sometimes we would drive through Bramwell to see the mansions of the coal barons or drive to Kimball to see Nonna. In the fall, we would just drive around looking at the fall leaves, which were colorful and plentiful.

In addition to Mother and Daddy smoking like chimneys, we would throw out any and all trash along the highway. It's just what everyone did then, and there was a lot of trash in the ditches. No handheld electronic games, we all talked or sang to the radio. When I talked too much or got to be too annoying, we had to play "Quaker's Meeting." The Quaker Meeting rule was simple. When the adult said go, the contest began. The one who sat still and said nothing the longest, won. I don't think it mattered who won, but the adults would get a few minutes of silence. I never won the game. On those two-lane, twisty roads, it was easy to get carsick, so sometimes I would sit up front on Mother's lap while she continued to smoke.

Our best Sunday drive was to the Mercer County airport near Bluefield. Piedmont Airlines flew in a couple of flights daily from Charleston, WV, Roanoke, VA, or Charlotte, NC. It always seemed to be magical to me because from there you could go to New York City or Washington, DC, in no time. The ritual was that we would go out to eat in Bluefield on Sunday afternoon. One time the *Sunset News* even printed the following: "Mr. and Mrs. Luke Gianato and daughters Martha and Jenna Lou dined at Pete's Restaurant on Sunday." Afterward, we would go to the airport in time for the four o'clock plane to land. We would stand at the chain-link fence right by the runway, and wait and wait to see the plane descend. Men in suits, ladies in high heels, hats, and gloves, and sometimes well-dressed children would parade off the plane. Then we watched the new passengers embark while Daddy treated us to a snow cone or ice cream. We watched the propellers rev up, the door close, and the plane turn around like a top, and then head down the runway, lifting off quickly through the mountains.

Not long ago, Martha met a former flight attendant of Piedmont—now US Air—who flew into Bluefield during the 1950s and 1960s. This seasoned flier said the landings and takeoffs in Bluefield would take your breath away because the ascents and descents were so sharp. With the steep, high mountains, pilots had little airspace to clear the mountaintops. She remembers very clearly having to sit on those narrow benches outside the terminal's ticket office waiting for takeoffs and landings. She also watched the people who stood by the chain-link fence to watch the planes take off and land. So we watched them, and they watched us. Funny, don't you think?

The first four-lane highway I can remember riding on was in 1957, when I was eleven years old. Dad drove us all to Washington, DC, for the burial of Mother's oldest brother, Lewis, at Arlington National Cemetery. A career naval man, Uncle Lewis and his family had lived in Florida. A Cooke by name, Uncle Lewis was naval head cook on many naval vessels. Getting to Washington was a sad trip for us all, but also an adventure for me. I was impressed with the flat, straight roads and those with more than two lanes. Mother hated all the congestion, but I was amazed that cars could ride side by side and not wreck. A cold day in the Capital City, it was the first time I had heard a military gun salute and witnessed the presentation of the American flag.

CHAPTER 25

Children Should Be Seen and Not Heard

On several Christmases, Aunt Gladys and Uncle Bill (her second husband) would drive from Washington, Pennsylvania for the holiday. Uncle Bill's favorite saying was, "No worries, snow flurries, tomorrow is Christmas." The big surprise one Christmas was that they brought us a dog we named Pepper. He was the brother of their dog, Fritz. Mother would never even think of keeping a dog inside the house. Arlene Blevins was the only person we knew growing up that kept an inside dog. Uncle Bill built him a doghouse while he was there. We kept Pepper chained on a stake around the doghouse. Of course, Pepper was always barking at the Giardina's cats. When it got really cold and snowy, Mother would take the dog on its leash to the basement. Naturally, the dog never knew how to walk on a leash and would always pull and tug. Daddy let Pepper loose every Sunday morning to let him run, and run he did! He chased every car going up and down to Crumpler. He would run out of sight and then speed back down the road. Daddy got a big charge watching him bark and run as fast as the cars were going. That dog would be only inches away from the tires of the cars. Daddy always said Pepper could run as fast as the cars since he had been on his yard chain all week. After a while, Daddy would holler, "Here boy, here boy." Of course everyone in Elkridge could hear him, and Mother would be embarrassed.

Another time, Aunt Gladys and Uncle Bill came for Christmas with a ping-pong table for a gift. We set it up in the "freezer room," and we all learned to play. Daddy was especially good at serving the ball with his special "English" technique. As much as I adored Aunt Gladys, I did get in hot water with her that Christmas. After I was chattering and chattering, she said something like, "Children should be seen and not heard." I then proceeded to call her a "square." Now that term was quite fashionable in the mid-1950s, meaning someone that was old-fashioned. Actually, she was quite offended. I thought it was funny, and she usually laughed at my stupid comments, but this time she did not. As I remember, about three weeks after her visit, Mother received a newspaper article from Aunt Gladys. She wrote in bright blue ink, "Read this to Jenna Lou." Well I was offended, because she knew I could read. Anyway it was like an advice column in which an adolescent had called an adult a square. I think the gist of it was that an apology was due to the adult. We kidded about it for a long time, but I did make amends, and didn't refer to any adult from that point on as a square.

Another Christmas tradition we had was a musical one. Martha played the piano from her sheet music, and all of us would sing the standard Christmas carols, even Mother. During the singing, I am sure I threw in a little dance or two!

Chapter 26

School Rituals

The start of school every fall was a big deal—that is, for us girls. A new school year meant a few new clothes, provided we had grown during the summer. Bluefield was our shopping mecca. Thornton's and A.W. Cox Department Stores were our favorites. If we behaved, Mother rewarded us by letting us x-ray our feet in Cox's shoe department stand-alone x-ray machine—a source of entertainment rather than anything medical. It worked like this: you put one foot into the slot, just like standing on a scale, pushed a side button, a bright light came on, and low and behold, you saw all the bones in that foot. Other foot, same process. One time wasn't enough, so we x-rayed our feet over and again.

Trying shoes for size was easy. Mother didn't have to do the thumb-at-the-end-of-your-toe test. We just put on the new shoe and x-rayed our foot. If the shoe fit, we wore it. It is a wonder adults our age haven't had serious foot diseases from overexposure to x-rays. Shoes bought, we walked then to Kresge's luncheonette counter for a hamburger lunch.

New clothes aside, the biggest hunt each and every fall was for schoolbooks. Every kid from first through twelfth grade had to buy school textbooks and workbooks along with other school supplies such as paper, pencils, and crayons. Now the crayons became status symbols. A kid was really something if he had a Crayola 24-count box, as opposed to the regular 8-count box. No one we ever knew had any kind of crayons other than Crayolas.

Our bookstore in Northfork was the back, right, two shelves in the G.C. Murphy Five and Dime Store. Grade school had the bottom shelves and grades seven through twelve had the top. Parents and children alike could walk down the aisles, looking and leafing through pages to get a jump-start on what would be taught that year. Looking back, this leafing and looking were our only curriculum guides.

No one purchased books right away. The skill was to wait until the very last day before school opened to buy books. Second-, third-, or fourth-hand books were handed down by brothers or sisters. If purchased from friends, the cost was pennies on the dollar.

Schools issuing free texts or having class sets did not become a reality for years. The local PTA bought books for those kids who could not afford them. This, of course, was done very privately. Mother was in charge of this project the years she was Mrs. PTA. We always wanted to know who got these freebies, but Mother would never tell us.

More kudos for Mom: I can honestly say we don't remember a single day when Mother wasn't there to greet us when we came home from school. Every day! We were secure in that manner.

Chapter 27

I Am A Blue Bird

Situated between Rt. 52 and the N&W Railroad—now Norfolk Southern—Northfork Grade School included grades one through six. With no such thing as kindergarten, I begged and begged Mother to let me start first grade when I was five years old. Probably for her own sanity, Mother finally agreed. So in September 1952 I entered first grade, where I met Judy and Clara Lambie, two gals who have remained lifelong friends. Our teacher, Mrs. Wilson, was the perfect first-grade teacher. She always had her hair styled at Linda's Beauty Shop and her nails painted red. I liked Mrs. Wilson; she made us all feel important.

Of all the goals for first graders, learning to read was Priority Number One. While mastering this, we kids learned quickly what grouping meant in education. In our classroom we had three groups—Blue Birds, Red Birds, and Yellow Birds. Or more to the point, fast readers, medium readers, and slow readers sprang to life. Of course no kid ever said anything, but we just knew who was a good reader and who was not. Interestingly, those reading groups followed us all through grade school. Rigid rules surrounded reading groups. I remember very well getting in hot water for talking out of turn in reading circle. Guess what? When I got home, I got in hot water number two.

In the West Virginia mountains, we had long, cold winters. Our school clothes were heavy coats, hats, and scratchy wool leggings under our dresses. These leggings—the long-ago forerunners to tights—matched our coats, had suspenders, and I hated them. Girls just did not wear long pants in the 1950s, only dresses. That came later with Women's Lib. In the cold and snow, kids often wore boots and galoshes, either brown or black. We girls would love it when our classmate Jimmie Hubbard would help us take off our galoshes in the coatroom. There hung all our coats, our lunch boxes, and our other school stuff, and on the floor, he set our galoshes.

Martha was now a sixth grader. Daddy drove us to school and dropped us off each morning, but in the afternoon, we walked home. Mother preferred we walk beside the railroad tracks instead of the "busy" main road. Poor Martha, her job was to take care of me and keep me safe. Usually at some point a freight train—coal fired, not diesel—rumbled by us gathering steam to pull the grade for Bluefield. The train soot and cinders would cover everything. When we got home, my little white socks would have black soot and cinders on them. In addition, my socks would have the print of the strap from my Mary Jane shoes. We would have to be careful walking in the gravel along the railroad tracks. If we fell down, which happened often, we would scrape and cut our arms and legs enough to have our wounds covered with that red Mercurochrome that lasted for days. Besides the gravel hazard, we walkers also carried our homework, books, and notebooks in our arms, which usually kept us off balance. There were no such things as backpacks, and the book bags that looked like luggage were for sissies.

Like most schools, even today, lunchtime was a special time in our school day. We would take out our metal lunch boxes and eat in our classroom. Kids could purchase small cartons of Foremost Milk or buy any kind of soft drink. We all ate peanut butter and jelly sandwiches regularly, and no one had food allergies. That was something we never heard of. Every day after lunch, before we went outside to play, we eagerly awaited the long cabinet that would be pulled from a hallway closet. It was the candy store, a PTA moneymaking project. We all lined up, bought our candy, and went off to play.

Chapter 28

Color in the Lines

Mrs. Goble was my second-grade teacher; she was old and her voice wobbly. When we played outside at recess or after lunch, she and most of the teachers smoked cigarettes. They stood with their kerchiefs on their heads, smoking, talking, and laughing.

This was the year all the grade-school kids got the polio vaccine. It was still experimental, but somehow McDowell County children were recipients. There was a far-reaching campaign to make certain all children were given the series of vaccine shots. Mother, who was president of the PTA, and the other PTA parents were busy ensuring that all the parents were educated on the need to vaccinate all children since polio was so widespread. After I completed my series of vaccines, I received a card from the National Foundation for Infantile Paralysis, which stated, "Jenna Lou Gianato has been enrolled as a Polio Pioneer and this certificate of membership is hereby presented for taking part in the first national tests of a trial polio vaccine conducted during 1954." Kids also participated in the March of Dimes campaigns, collecting dimes to go to the cause. As a result of these campaigns, polio in the United States is no longer the dreaded disease it once was. We were proud that our little county in southern West Virginia helped to make it happen.

I loved Mrs. Reed in the third grade. She wore lots of rings, had a deep booming voice, and played the piano. I loved for her to play for us. We would join her with the rhythm band, our triangles, drums, and tambourines. That year I went to see Dr. Blaydes, a well-known eye doctor in Bluefield. I had a lazy eye and had to wear glasses. Imagine how I looked as a third grader: skinny as a rail, losing teeth and growing new ones, and wearing glasses with one clear lens and one darkened lens. Eventually that lazy eye did straighten out. That was the year I took piano lessons, and unlike Martha, I hated sitting on the piano bench. I would rather dance to the rhythm than make the music.

One thing was certain about grade school in Northfork. We had to color in the lines and use real-life colors—no green sky, no orange bananas, and no pink basketballs. We never explored our inner selves.

The only time we remember most folks going to the dentist was to get a tooth pulled because of a toothache, or to have all of their teeth pulled so they could get false ones. Having straight, perfect teeth wasn't common. Somehow Martha and I were blessed with straight, white teeth while some of our friends had crooked or buckteeth. However, no one seemed to think anything about it. No one had dental insurance. Mother did take us for checkups, but that was the exception rather than the rule.

Chapter 29

To Kentucky and Back

For my fourth-and fifth-grade years, we moved to Ashland, Kentucky. Mom and Dad were having their usual problems, but Daddy got a good job as general manager of Jack Moses' Ford dealership. Ashland was really different since we didn't have those high mountains, and it was usually foggy because Ashland was set on the shores of the Ohio River. My fourth-grade teacher, Mrs. Reeves, and fifth-grade teacher, Mrs. Duncan, were both terrific. One day Mrs. Duncan sent home a note to my mother. The only thing I knew was this note was not for the boys—just the girls. My mother had to give me permission to do something; she said no. So the day all the other girls in my class went to learn something special, I stayed in the room with the boys. I remember clearly how Mrs. Duncan just shook her head in disbelief that Mother did not let me attend. The only thing Mother told me was that I was too young and immature to learn about the topic. Of course I moped around, so she did let me buy a new green notebook to cheer myself up. I guess that goes back to the idea of the "egg hatching behind the colored church."

Martha was a ninth grader, a majorette in the Putnam Junior High Band, excelling in her class work, and getting prettier and prettier. She always remembers classmate Ernie Brown and his performance in the school's Annual Spring Talent Show. He was a country singer. Ernie stood center stage, strummed his guitar a couple times, tilted his head towards Martha, strummed again, and announced to the entire school and faculty, "I'm dedicating this country ditty to that little booger sitting right there." He then pointed directly at her and yelled out, "Miss Martha." Ernie's singing was good, but my sister saw none of his performance since she had slunk down in her seat, completely out of sight. Martha said she always wondered if Ernie made it big in Nashville. Of course, she was known as "The Little Booger" the rest of the school year.

Martha loved Ashland High School, took part in many clubs, and made wonderful friends. She loved learning Spanish from Señor Creech. No longer a puzzle, English studies just clicked in under her tenth-grade English teacher, Mrs. Kenney. Those were two interests that carried over into college, and ultimately into her teaching career. That was also the year she met Dick Mateer, probably her first boyfriend. No wonder then she cried most of the way back to Northfork that summer following her sophomore year.

Daddy got his own Pontiac dealership back in Northfork by the end of the school year in 1957, and we moved back to the very same house in Elkridge. Pete Capadini even repainted all the rooms the way we had them before we moved, and told Mother she was moving back into his dream house. Mother replied she was happy to be back, but said, "I wish you had dreamed bigger bedrooms." For two thousand dollars and Mother's 1955 aqua and white Chevrolet Coupe, Luke Gianato was in business.

Chapter 30

Luke's Ice Box

Martha and I learned a lot about people and human nature because we hung around the showroom at the dealership. Daddy treated all customers equally, wanting to sell his vehicles to every customer who came through the door. Old, young, white, colored, it didn't matter. He also genuinely liked people, and because of this, people gravitated to him. A free spirit by nature, I was grounded in practical and conventional rules of Northfork and of the times. I did learn to be an observer of people, and to converse with the young, old, smart, dumb, or uppity people. As a matter of practicality, I learned to become detailed, which would prove tactical in years to come during my career at FedEx.

Always the trader, Daddy was creative in the down payments on a car. He would accept diamond rings, ponies, and guns—anything of value to make the deal. He had some crackerjack salesmen. I thought all salesmen were party folks, loved the women, and were supposed to be very outgoing. Some of the local men just liked to loaf around at the dealership. During all the years Martha and I hung out or worked at the dealership, we were always treated with respect—they knew Daddy would kill them if not.

One of Daddy's employees was Bob Norris, his service manager and all-around good guy at the dealership. Bob was a young man in 1957 when he went to work for Daddy and earned his "degree," as he called it, at "Gianato Tech." Daddy always trusted Bob, and Bob spent his working years at Daddy's dealerships.

In the early Northfork days, Daddy had a very small office built for him in the back of the showroom. Back then, buildings did not have central air conditioning, and very few people had any type of air conditioning. Daddy had a portable air conditioner in the office, and we all said people ended up buying cars on hot days because it was so comfortable in there. We also said he kept it shivering cold when it wasn't hot so customers would quickly sign on the dotted line just to get out of there and warm up! Behind his back, employees fondly called his office "Luke's Ice Box."

CHAPTER 31

Princesses of the Bus Station

The Trailways Bus Line had its Northfork bus station directly off the right, front corner of Dad's Pontiac dealership. A perfect location for bus passengers, it was easy access since all the little towns fed into Northfork at this time. Daddy's secretary, Aneita Oliver, sold bus tickets in addition to all of her other responsibilities. When she was out of the office for vacation, lunch, or on Saturdays, Martha and I would work as bus-station agents. The bus station was our first job. We learned life skills there. But Martha, because she was older, learned them first.

I started working the bus station around the age of eleven. Standing on two old, Coca-Cola crates to reach the counter, I learned geography up close and personal. I could look up and write a ticket to anywhere in the continental United States—many of them to New York, Cleveland, Columbus, and Washington, DC. My desk was a long board, and long racks of rubber stamps were mounted on the wall above it, each with the name of a city, and stacks of ticket forms. For each stop the bus made, I had to stamp the city's name on a section of the ticket. To write a ticket to Washington, DC, for example, I had to stamp, "Bluefield, Roanoke, Staunton, Arlington, Washington, DC." After all the cities and stops were stamped or filled in, the bus driver would tear the ticket on a perforated line at its particular destination.

Writing a bus ticket was a snap compared to making change. Should a ticket cost $18.50, and I was given $20, I could subtract and give the correct change. Usually that operation I could do in my head. The problem surfaced when a rider wanted a ticket and waited until the bus pulled in to buy one. Many times folks would stand outside just in case somebody could give them a ride. Figuring out change in a timely manner with last-minute customers and a hurry-up bus driver did cause delays for everyone and major panic for me. One such time the rider bought a ticket to Bluewell costing 65 cents. I couldn't figure change fast enough for the one dollar he handed me, so I just asked, "How much change do you want back?" Daddy overheard this and had a major fit. As a result, I had to memorize all the change combinations for one dollar, five dollars, and ten dollars. The last thing Daddy wanted was to be the bus ticket agent while he was selling a car. We girls really had to know what we were doing. Besides, we never wanted to disappoint Daddy. So to solve my math dilemma, my smart, math friend Judy would visit me at work. She was really fast at making correct change.

We became so proficient that we could write bus tickets to faraway cities and could also write bus-line transfers. I once sent a traveler to Los Angeles and had him transfer from Trailways Bus Lines to the Greyhound Bus Lines. Now this was a challenge since I not only wrote the ticket but also had to know how to read the Greyhound schedules. Thankfully Greyhound used gray tickets, and Trailways used gold. It was fun playing grown-up, doing things like calling the Ashland Oil station at the end of town to tell them Trailways had just dropped their truck part off at the bus station. Looking back on our first jobs now, we both wished we had kept those racks of city stamps and rolls of old tickets.

Even with all we learned as ticket agents, we were never as good as Aneita Oliver. Along with being Trailways ticket agent and secretary, she ran Dad's office. She kept the books, answered phones, and coordinated all the day-to-day activities of the dealership. But the bus station became very important the day she sold a bus ticket to one fellow named Jack Pickett, who jokingly said over the years, "I should have just sued Trailways Bus Lines," but instead he married his love, Aneita.

CHAPTER 32

Mr. Truman Waves His Hat

In 1957—during my sixth-grade year—I attended my first Veterans Day parade in Welch, our county seat. The Welch Veterans Day festivity was a big event for the county and southern West Virginia, and has been for more than ninety years. The parade always featured area bands, civic-sponsored floats, and dignitaries in convertibles. The tradition was special that year since I saw the thirty-third president of the United States, Harry S. Truman. That was the first time I saw a president! Some years before, Mr. Truman had become friends with Sam Solins, a prominent local lawyer and organizer of the Veterans Day event.

Now Mr. Solins was a very special person. According to Daddy, Mr. Solins and twelve other West Virginians headed to St. Louis, Missouri, after World War I. These veterans met with other World War I veterans from around the country. This group included Harry S. Truman, and through their efforts and influences, these veterans founded what became the American Legion.

From this interaction, Mr. Solins and the future president established their friendship. Eventually at Mr. Solins invitation, President Truman joined the list of acclaimed dignitaries that have come back each and every November 11 to the small town of Welch, to prove to the state and the nation that every veteran from every war and conflict are true heroes in West Virginia.

Martha was marching, playing her saxophone. As Mr. Truman passed us on the parade route in a convertible, he waved his hat in his right hand and showed a big smile. As Mr. Truman passed by, Daddy said, "He is the reason World War II ended." This meant nothing to me at the time since I just wanted to see Martha marching along.

Chapter 33

Learn Your Counties and County Seats!

At one time, Daddy was president of the Kiwanis Club, Martha was president of the junior class, and I was president of the sixth-grade class. Woodrow Helms, our teacher, made sure I learned and used parliamentary procedure to conduct class meetings, which occurred once a month. He was the best teacher I ever had. I had to work hard, learned to write cursive beautifully, and loved to participate in spelling bees. Mr. Helms was also the grade school principal and the dad of my best friend Judy. He was a very strict disciplinarian.

West Virginia history was important to Mr. Helms. Every sixth-grade student had to learn, pronounce, spell, and identify every county and county seat in the state of West Virginia. That meant fifty-five counties, and fifty-five county seats. On the outlined map that hung in the front of our classroom, each student—when their name was called—marched to the front of the room, picked up Mr. Helms' pointer, and identified the location, the name of the county, and the county seat. Big stuff!

Every Friday we had a spelling test, a math test, and wrote a composition on some topic Mr. Helms chose. If a student's composition and handwriting were good, he would post them on the bulletin board in the hallway. On a lighter side, we sang a lot of songs in class. When we went to recess, Mr. Helms smoked his cigarettes while rolling the ball for us in kick-pen soccer. After I finished college, Mr. Helms gave me a folder that had all my important papers from grades one through six. He made an impact on many, many students and teachers throughout the years. Mr. Helms bought Chevrolets from Carroll's.

It was during that time a big flu epidemic hit. Mother got really sick. I remember Remmie taking care of her. Mother didn't have to go to the doctor; the doctor came to our home. Dr. Ficken was formerly a coal company doctor. When the coal companies started to consolidate, Dr. Ficken went into private practice. He would arrive with his doctor bag, check Mother's heart and lungs, and give her some pills. Anytime we got sick, he would come. In later years, we would have to go to his office in Kimball because he stopped making house calls. If we knocked on the side door, Aunt Mary, his nurse, would let us into the office. Dr. Ficken smoked a lot of Lucky Strikes. He smoked while he examined patients, and his ashtray was always running over. Nonetheless, he was an excellent doctor, and served our area successfully for years. Dr. Ficken bought cars from Daddy.

Pictured at the stoplight in Northfork in 1957 is Gianato Pontiac Sales and the Trailways Bus Station.

Pictured here posing on the playground of Northfork Grade School are some classmates during their sixth-grade recess. First row, left to right, are Jenna Lou and Linda Prillaman. Second row, left to right, are Judy Helms, Clara Lambie Keesee, and Mary Krulatz.
Photo Courtesy of Judy Helms Sargent

All dressed up in their summer attire at the house in Northfork, Jenna Lou and Martha returned from another summer vacation at the Colonial Inn in Myrtle Beach.

Chapter 34

Fake Prom? Real Prom?

While I was busy presiding over the sixth-grade class meetings, Martha, being junior-class president, and officers Vickie Hylton, Peggy Alley, and Barbara Ann Lambert had to coordinate all the efforts for a successful prom. It was tradition that the junior class always presented the prom, meaning all the work to produce the event fell on the shoulders of the junior class.

Finishing the yearbook that year was a hassle, trying to meet the publisher's deadline and still getting in the important stuff, like the senior prom pictures, class wills, and class history. Well, the yearbook staff never made that deadline because it was much too early for the end-of-the-year events in May, including the prom. So Martha said they solved the problem! The seniors and the senior superlatives—the "bests" as voted by the senior class—and a few juniors, all dressed up in their finest: the girls in party dresses, and the boys in suits and ties. Everyone gathered in the Little Auditorium outside Miss Vecellio's typing room, and posed as if they were dancing. Richard Perdue even tapped Jack Grose on the shoulder, pretending he was cutting in to dance with Carole Wallace. Jimmy Mahady tapped Billy McCormick, who was dancing with Nancy Sheffield, and Jackie Willis cut in on Bill Henthorne and Martha's dance. The class history and the class will didn't make it into the yearbook, but were read aloud at Class Night prior to the seniors' graduation. And so the prom was a success, but the prom photo in the yearbook was a fake.

Chapter 35

How We Loved Myrtle Beach

Some things remained constant for several decades. As a rule, McDowell County residents went to Myrtle Beach every summer and purchased a new car every three to four years. Dad's dealerships profited from that constant. Through the years, our family vacationed in Myrtle Beach at the Colonial Inn, "our summer home." We loved the owners, Joe and Evelyn Moses, and considered them family. I found a $320 cancelled check from the 1950s that Mother had written for our two-week stay at the Colonial Inn. That included lodging, two connecting rooms with a bath, and three meals a day for four people. What a deal! Of course, back then that was a good bit of money. When we were small, Mother hired colored women to take care of us while we were there. Those poor folks; they were not allowed to go to the ocean, except on Sunday nights. That rule made no sense to me even then. Otherwise, they were not allowed on the beach, in any restaurants, or in any hotels. In South Carolina, there were "colored" and "white" bathrooms too. In fact, I never saw any colored person in a restaurant or in a bathroom at home either, and they sat in the back of the bus as well.

One summer we were especially excited. Daddy spent a day down at the Court House in Conway—Myrtle Beach's county seat—researching a deed. Supposedly our grandfather had purchased choice real estate around 1920, and Daddy wanted to check it out. Unfortunately, the taxes were not paid after his dad died, and the land was forfeited. At that time, Daddy could have paid the taxes and gotten the land back, but he passed it up. Of course, that was before the big building boom at the beach—did we ever regret that!

We loved going to the beach in the morning, eating a delicious lunch, and then going back to the beach in the afternoon. We always rented an umbrella, chairs, and floats for the time we were there. If it rained, we had to occupy our time on the porch with crayons, coloring books, and rocking chairs—all of which I hated. Dinner at the Colonial Inn had two sittings. We always ate early, around five o'clock. Dinner attire included dresses for Martha, Mother, and me. I always had to have hair bows made of satin ribbon that matched the color of my dress. Matching socks and dressy, patent-leather shoes were also a must. Daddy wore a coat and tie for dinner. After dinner we would go to the Pavilion, the local amusement park, and ride as many carnival rides as time permitted. I had to sit and be as patient as possible while Mother played bingo at Jones' Bingo. She played two cards, and when the numbers were called, she put a piece of corn down to cover the number on her card. A number of times, Mother hollered "Bingo!" after only a few numbers had been called. Everyone would groan, and the caller would say, "Hold your cards, there is a problem. Only three numbers have been called." Once again, I had jiggled around and gotten her cards out of sorts. Of course, I was again in hot water! Near the bingo hall was an auction house. Mother and Daddy liked to go; however, I was threatened with my life if I moved or talked—another Quaker Meeting moment. They were afraid they would end up bidding on some unwanted item.

Sometimes we would go to the beach for a week, and then Daddy would fly down for the second week. One year Dad caught the Piedmont airplane in Bluefield and transferred in Charlotte, NC, for the leg to Myrtle Beach. After he boarded the plane in Charlotte, the pilot announced, "Ladies and Gentlemen, the plane is overloaded, and we cannot take off. We need our heaviest passenger to take another flight." Since Daddy was in his "two-plenty" stage, they threw him off. Was he ever hot! He had to catch the Greyhound Bus to the beach. Since he was a stockholder of Piedmont, he wrote quite a letter to the Piedmont Airlines President emphasizing his displeasure in having to take the bus to Myrtle Beach. Needless to say, he sold his stock.

When we were older, Mother took Martha and me to see *Gone with the Wind*, a reissued movie in the early 1960s. It was our first *Gone with the Wind*, and our first in an air-conditioned theater. It just couldn't get any better than that! Myrtle Beach will always be special.

Chapter 36

Name Reality Check

The first time I remember my name being mispronounced was on my first day at Elkhorn–Northfork Junior High School, which included grades seven through nine. Not only did the kids from Northfork attend the E–N Junior High, but kids from other grade schools too. The school was located on Rt. 52, about six miles from Northfork on the twisty, narrow, mountainous roads going toward Bluefield. It was the old, white Elkhorn High School before Northfork and Elkhorn consolidated. The high school mascot was the Blue Demons, and the junior high, the Little Demons. When all the buses arrived—and all kids came by bus—everyone assembled in the gymnasium. There were no seats for students on the floor because the faculty sat there, so all the students sat up high in the bleachers.

Of course, the students from Northfork sat together checking out the kids from Crumpler and Elkhorn. The principal called out each class, and then that class would walk out with its homeroom teacher. Mr. Goosens, the principal, started out with 7-A, supposedly including all the kids who got into the band. Judy and I were not called. He then called out 7-B, nonband students. Once again, Judy and I were not called. He then called out 7-C, which were some of the kids who would eventually get in the band. He called out "Jenny Lou Guy-and-toe," mispronouncing my name so badly that I did not think it was mine. Anyway, I was in shock that I didn't get into 7-A, and then mortified and embarrassed that my name could have been that mess that Mr. Goosens called out. I didn't know what to do when all the seventh grades had left. I finally got up and went down to the floor where the teachers were sitting. Of course, the eighth and ninth graders were watching when I said my name wasn't called. I was so embarrassed, but it was finally straightened out, and I went to the 7-C classroom. Apparently Mr. Goosens was not from our side of the county, but he did start buying cars from Daddy. Luckily, both Judy and I were moved into 7-A in January when we got into the band. For Christmas that year I got a new flute, which I played for the next six years.

Seemed like we did a lot of oral reading in every class. We went down the rows student by student, paragraph by paragraph. No one ever listened to the reader because everyone was counting paragraphs and figuring out which one they would have to read out loud. Boring! We also did a lot of memorizing and reciting to class members. The two things I remember best were the Preamble to the Constitution and the Gettysburg Address. We spent weeks and weeks on those projects, and every student had to recite standing in front of the classroom. If you were the reciter in this case, you could look out at your classmates and see almost every one mouthing the words as you said the passage aloud.

Chapter 37

Twixt and Tween Years

It was during Mrs. Riggs' reading class that we learned about the Russians going into space. Even in McDowell County the focus would become science and math. During that time, we read in the *Welch Daily News* that some young boys from a county school, Big Creek, headed up by Homer Hickam, were creating and shooting rockets. They went on to win the National Science Contest. By 1998, Homer and his friends were internationally known as the "Rocket Boys."

Formed five years before West Virginia became a state, McDowell County celebrated its centennial in 1958. Businesses and local civic groups organized countywide activities, contests, and special events. Posey Belcher, a Northfork businessman, headed up the activities for our end of the county. He owned the Northfork Hardware Store, and his wife owned Edna's Dress Shop. Neither of these two bought cars from Daddy; they always just walked down the hill to work. The big affair ran May 11-17, with a parade in Welch to honor the queen and her court. Dot Mitchell from Keystone won, which we loved since the chosen queen wasn't from Welch. Daddy got into the centennial spirit by joining the beard-growing contest. He didn't win, and on more than one occasion Mother said, "Luke, I never did like a man with a beard."

I was still the littlest and the skinniest, but the kids seemed to like me. I got involved with school activities, was selected cheerleader, and did just fine changing classes and being the low man on the totem pole. By eighth grade, we were in the swing of things and busy with the newspaper, Sub Deb Club, Honor Society, and cheerleading. Several of us got to go with the ninth graders on their ninth-grade trip since there was extra room on the bus. We went to Washington, DC, sleeping overnight on the bus. We changed our clothes in the bus station the next morning and had breakfast. We toured the Bureau of Engraving and Printing, the Smithsonian, and then I was one of the kids who climbed the Washington Monument—all fifty flights of stairs with twenty-five steps per flight. I loved the Wax Museum, but my very favorite was the U.S. Capitol. Can you imagine that we toured the U.S. Capitol by ourselves, with no guide and no capitol security? This included the private subway and the Senate Room. The Lincoln and Jefferson Memorials were next, and then we got back on the bus. We did all of that in one day!

We were twixt and tween during those years and said stupid things to each other like, "If your nose is runny, and you think it's funny, well it's snot." In Northfork, the Marilyn Monroe body was in, not Audrey Hepburn. Of course, I wasn't Marilyn. We girls sat under sunlamps to get a tan, wore leg makeup when the sunlamp didn't work, and wore sack dresses. We ordered a spring-hinged device to squeeze our boobs, making them appear bigger, and wore necklaces with a big initial to represent our first name. We also loved when one of our parents would drive a group of us to the Kimball Roller Rink. While I managed to skate pretty well to the music, I never skated backward. On Saturday mornings, the big event for us girls was a Trailways bus trip to Welch—thirteen miles away—to the Pocahontas Theatre. WELC Radio Station held an on-the-air dance party. Although it was mostly for the Welch kids, we still hoped the Welch boys would ask us to dance. They seldom did. Next was window shopping in stores like Chris-Ann, comparing Welch's G.C. Murphy's to ours in Northfork, gazing in Davis Jewelry, and then eating at the Flat Iron Drugstore before catching the 3:30 p.m. bus back to Northfork. In athletics, the E–N Little Demons won the junior high county basketball tournament. We were so proud to be the champs!

Around this time, the transistor radio hit the stores, and naturally we all got one. It was great! We could carry our own personal radio around. We listened to local stations WELC, WHIS, and WOVE before six o'clock, but we loved when we could get WLS all the way from Chicago after nine o'clock at night. We learned all the new and popular songs, and fell asleep many nights to the tunes. Of course when we woke up in the morning, all we heard was static.

Chapter 38

N-E Class of 1959

Martha was a senior in high school and planned to go to college. For some reason, Mother had the idea that Davis and Elkins College, in the eastern part of West Virginia, was not only private but also very prestigious. The three of us drove there to check out the school. Mother loved it, but Martha was not extremely enthused. That was my first trip to a college campus, and I thought it was pretty nice. Mother did not want Martha to go to Concord College—the local teacher's college in southern West Virginia—because most all college students in our area did. Of course, Martha preferred Concord. So that conflict lasted about six months. At this point I didn't care because I was not on Mother's firing line.

Martha's senior year was a whirlwind of activity with heavy-duty classes, the yearbook, and college choices. Chemistry class was a mystery. She never quite understood the periodic table, but with Joe Arena's help, managed to make A's and B's. Added to this mix were her advanced math classes—Trig, Solid Geometry, and Calculus—from her favorite math teacher, Jennings Boyd. Mr. Boyd was the most outstanding math teacher in the state of West Virginia. Jennings Boyd bought cars from Daddy.

The Blue Demon yearbook staff and Martha, the editor, began planning the book's layout in late October. With suggestions from her yearbook sponsor and English/Latin teacher, Mrs. Powell, Martha and the yearbook staff were determined to plan a yearbook in which the entire senior class would have major input, and that the student body would be proud. They decided to include the Class Will, the Class History, and the Class Prophecy in the *1959 Blue Demon*. It was a first! The wills featured items from the seniors, which bordered on the humorous or the ridiculous, that were willed to juniors. A blonde beauty with a fashion model's look, Janice Blankenship willed "my excess fat to Sandra Crouch." Another read, "I, Vickie Hylton, will my cheerleading uniform to Paul Forrest if he will promise not to burst the seams." Or, "I, Mackie Oliver, will my Phys. Ed. clothes to Terry Treolo if he will wash them." Also, "I, Juanita Witt, will my seat in Mr. Trechock's Democracy class to Louise Taylor."

The assignment of the Class History went to three smart, young men. Entitled "The Class of 1959," it offered the history of the students from grade school and through their senior year, and was set in the theme of the then-popular TV show *Dragnet*. It began "This is the school! Northfork–Elkhorn High School. We work here. We are students. Our names, Carl Porter, Joe Arena, and Ray Decker. Our job, to reveal how this graduation class was assembled." From here, the guys traced each senior and their connection to school in *Dragnet* fashion. It was cleverly done and reminded them all how they came from different directions to become friends.

Titled "Excursions Around the World," the Class Prophecy was set in 1969—a piece of pure fiction. It projected a theme of space exploration, something that was just beginning to become a reality in our lives.

The yearbook was delivered in late May. Excited, the yearbook staff and the student body huddled in groups—autographing pages, writing their good-byes, and filling up pages of memories. Thinking back, Martha wished they could have incorporated the excitement and captured the joy of the 1958-59 basketball team going to the Class AA playoffs in Huntington. It was a first for Northfork–Elkhorn, but not the last! Remember in years to come, Jennings Boyd ended up holding the state's basketball championship record.

Three days—May 17, May 19, and May 21—quickly ended Martha's senior year. May 17 was baccalaureate, with several local preachers conducting their ceremony in the school gym. Two days later came Class Night, a Northfork-Elkhorn tradition, held with the entire town in attendance. A fun night, various seniors made announcements of special awards and athletic accolades. The Class Will, the Class History, and the Class Prophecy were read, and the choir rendered musical selections, including "I'm Forever Blowing Bubbles." Remmie was in town at the time, and we all dressed up to enjoy the evening.

Graduation came two days later. Dr. Cloyd Armbrister, Concord College Business Department Chair and our band director's brother, delivered the commencement address. The family was so proud when Martha achieved "Highest Honors" in her class, and was even voted Most Likely to Succeed. Mr. Painter, our principal, presented the class to Mr. I. J. Powell, assistant superintendent of McDowell County Schools, who then presented diplomas to the seniors. Classmates Vickie Hylton and Bob Watson received the Good Citizenship Awards, while Barbara Helen Lambert and Martha were recognized as Outstanding English Students. All in all, within those three days, Martha said they prayed, played, and graduated.

Martha was busy that summer, working at the bus station and getting ready to go to college at Concord. She won out when she convinced

Mother that her goal was to be a teacher, and Concord was the best place for her to achieve that goal. Because of the ongoing feud, her decision for Concord was late. All the dorm rooms were full. She stayed her first year in a private home on Faculty Hill, and Mother was thrilled that Martha wasn't rooming in the dorm. How much safer would she be living across the street from Miss Wilson, Dean of Women, between her Spanish professor and her American History professor, and three doors up from Dr. Marsh, president of Concord College? To Martha, it was like being in a classroom around the clock, but she loved Concord and does to this day. It was strange to be by myself for the first time. I was then the focus of attention—positive and negative!

CHAPTER 39

A Personal Wave from Mr. Kennedy

Martha was a freshman at Concord, and I was in the ninth grade. For me, that brought cheerleading and every other activity at school. Besides being head cheerleader, banner carrier for the band, and in the National Junior Honor Society, I enjoyed the Sub Deb Club.

The 1960 national presidential election was the first time I paid any attention to politics. John Kennedy was the reason. The fact that he was Catholic, handsome, and a Democrat was reason enough. The state Democratic primaries in May of 1960, proved to be a national battleground in West Virginia due to the Catholic issue. Kennedy had been in the area during the late 1950s giving speeches, and he attracted local attention. Local politicians known in McDowell County to support the "highest bidder" flocked to Kennedy because his campaign was rumored to have deep pockets. Rumors even had it that some official alone pocketed forty thousand dollars.

A big day for us was when the Kennedy campaign made a swing through the county. Hubert Humphrey, senator from Minnesota, had already been in Northfork and even parked his campaign bus in front of Daddy's dealership. Mrs. Helms told Judy and me that Kennedy was not scheduled to stop in Northfork, only in Keystone and Kimball. Why we didn't go there, who knows! Disappointed, we knew the his motorcade would be coming up Rt. 52 from Keystone and pass right by Judy's house. Judy and I decided to make signs, get cheerleader shakers, and attract the motorcade as it passed by. We worked all day on our signs, taped them to the side of her house, practiced our cheers, and patiently awaited the caravan. Based on the schedule printed in the *Welch Daily News*, the caravan was way late. We waited, waited, and waited.

Finally we saw the caravan approaching. Kennedy was not in the first car or in the second. By this time, we were yelling our cheers, shaking our shakers, and jumping around. Kennedy was in the third car! He was in the middle of the front seat, but turned around and waved to us with that big smile. We about died with excitement! We thought we were hot stuff, and couldn't wait to tell everyone that Kennedy waved to us personally. We got the wind knocked out of our sails when Daddy came home for supper and said Kennedy stopped right in front of the dealership, got out, and walked down to G.C. Murphy's, shaking hands with half the people we knew. Even worse was that Kennedy stopped right in front of Nonna's store in Kimball and held my young cousin, Michael, in his arms. As a result, Michael and Uncle Mike were pictured in *Look* magazine with Kennedy. That didn't discourage us very long though.

Election Day 1960 was special. It was a little windy and cold, but sunny. There was no school that day since West Virginia schools were polling places. Judy and I met Clara Lambie Keesee and Mary Krulatz to check out the new lipstick, new records, and magazines in G.C. Murphy's. The streets were busy, and there was an excitement in the air. After we did our important shopping, we went to the Curb-In for lunch and vowed we would all meet every four years on Election Day for lunch, no matter how old we got. We never did.

Chapter 40

Kennedy Frenzy

We fell in love with the Kennedys just like the kids did in the late 60s and 70s for the rock stars. Judy and I bought every book and magazine about the Kennedys we could get our hands on, and started a collection. Judy's mother even told my mother she was worried we were becoming fanatics. The day Kennedy was inaugurated, Judy stayed home from school claiming to have a sore throat. She watched the inauguration on television from the couch in her living room. I watched part of the inauguration during my lunch break on a television that the school set up for us students—the very first time we had a television on in our school. That was big stuff.

When the Kennedys were in the White House, we continued to be "fanatical" by buying anything Kennedy related—from Vaughn Meador albums to books and posters—anything. My favorite pastime was to write Jackie Kennedy, asking all kinds of questions from how she rolled her hair to where I should go to college. I got replies, usually from Letitita Baldrige, her social secretary. Typically I would be told, "work with school guidance counselors" (we didn't have any) "and your parents to help you select the right college." But I would be really excited when I got an envelope that had my name, address, and the White House return address on it. Before I could get to the post office box, Mamie, the postmistress, would say, "Jenna Lou, you have another letter from the White House." One time I wrote to the *Look* magazine editor in response to an article he had written about Jackie's French cousins. I told him how inspiring it was. To my surprise, my letter was published. We weren't the only ones catching the Kennedy bug. Many homes now had a picture of President Kennedy hanging in their living rooms beside the one they had of Franklin D. Roosevelt.

Judy and I wrote our ninth-grade term papers about their lives. Judy wrote about John, and I wrote about Jackie. The term paper was very formal, and we had to have footnotes and documentation of our research. We even got official, color portraits from the White House for our term-paper covers. I had Daddy's secretary type my term paper. We both got an A from Mary Thomason, our English teacher. She was so proud of our work that she said she laid them out along with her magazines on her coffee table when company came.

An interesting thing happened forty years later. I read Letitia Baldrige's biography and realized that her brother, Malcolm, had a National Quality Award named after him. While working at FedEx, I became heavily involved with FedEx's National Quality Award nomination process. When FedEx won, several other FedEx representatives and I were chosen to attend the presentation ceremony in Washington, DC. We witnessed FedEx Chairman of the Board, Fred Smith, receiving the award from President George H.W. Bush. I did not connect the dots at that time, but after reading Letitia's book—which contained her e-mail address—I sent her a message. Letitia responded. I told her I was one of those silly girls who wrote to the White House every week asking this or that. I also appreciated how positive all her correspondence had been.

She was most gracious with her response. So that was the closest contact I ever had with Jackie, my hero.

Chapter 41

Stupid Tricks and Other Misdemeanors

Mother declared her life was on hold because she took care of us girls. And that she did. I never did anything around the house—no dishes, no bed making, no ironing, no chores. My job was to make as many A's as possible on my report card, be polite to adults, get positive attention in public, and not embarrass the family. What other people thought was Mother's bottom line. Daddy just wanted me to learn and have fun, and he would take care of everything.

One time for sure I embarrassed the family. It was Christmastime and the Snow-in-a-Can just hit the shelves. It sprayed snow. Just think, having snow in a spray can! In the past, Mother let us do Christmas stencils on the windows with Glass Wax. I would take a stencil of a candy cane, hold the stencil against the windowpane, sponge Glass Wax onto the stencil, and have a decoration. After Christmas Mother would wipe off the Glass Wax, and the window would be clean. I bought an aerosol can of snow when Judy and I were downtown. I knew Mother would not let me use it on her windows on that very day, but Judy and I couldn't wait to try it out. On our way from town, we passed by the abandoned Coca-Cola building and sprayed our names on the green, wooden boards with the white snow—a really fun prank. After we sprayed our names, we tried to rub off the snow just like the Glass Wax. It didn't work. Rt. 52 was right there, and everyone going from Welch to Bluefield went right by that building and could easily see our names. We went on home, and all hell broke loose. Our mothers talked on the phone, and we got in major hot water. Of course I had to hear that "fools' names and fools' faces often appear in public places" among other choice bits of advice. It snowed over the next couple of days, so our snow names froze on the building and were up for more than a week for "God and everybody" to see them. Our parents made us scrub our names off in the cold. The funny part was, for years an imprint of our names remained, even after all that scrubbing.

Another Judy–Jenna Lou escapade happened when we played a trick on an underclassman. Her name was Lorie Baker, a young, impressionable seventh grader. She had gotten a D on her report card from Mrs. Hester, her math teacher. I was spending the night at Judy's on a Friday night, and without using good sense, we decided to call Lorie. Acting like Mrs. Hester and speaking with her thick, southern accent, I said in my best teacher voice, "This is Mrs. Hester, and I was looking over my grade book and found that I made a mistake on your report card; it should have been a B and not a D. See me Monday morning, and I will change your grade." Well, Lorie was in a lot of trouble with her parents over that D so she was very excited. As expected, Lorie went to Mrs. Hester on Monday morning, and Mrs. Hester had no idea what was going on. Lorie kept the D. We told Lorie we played the trick, which was stupid on our part. The water was so hot it was boiling!

Judy and I got smarter the next time we played a telephone trick. This time we were at my house. Earlier, Mother put in an extension telephone in a second-floor room that we used as a study. A little boy in Elkridge named Tommy Summers seemed like a fun target. We called from the upstairs telephone and told Tommy he had two secret admirers. As secret admirers, Judy and I told him he was cute and wanted to meet up with him at two o'clock on the front porch of Romeo's store. I remember he was very enthusiastic with the telephone call, so we thought we had him baited. We positioned ourselves on the platform at the bottom of our front porch steps, peering through the holes in the brick fence and watching at a distance for Tommy to appear at the store. Finally, we saw him walk up the alley beside the store, look around, and sit down on the bench. He looked like he had on his best shirt, and his hair was slicked back. He kept looking up and down the road to see if anyone was coming. The bad part was that we could not move because he would see us walking around. We had to stay crouched down, looking through the bricks. Of course we were laughing so hard we couldn't stop, but thank goodness he left after about fifteen minutes. Just as he was leaving, Mother came outside and wanted to know what we were doing lying on the sidewalk, staring through the fence, and laughing our heads off. We kept mum on the whole thing. So mum, in fact, I had forgotten the entire incident until Judy reminded me fifty years later!

Judy and I were the Nixon version of "dirty tricks" in Northfork. One of the few area Republicans, Mr. Hartell, the insurance man, had a "Vote Straight Republican" bumper sticker on his car. We found a "Humphrey" sticker during the 1960 primaries and stuck it on top of his Republican sticker. I do think quite a few grown-ups thought it was funny, but since Mr. Hartell purchased Pontiacs from Daddy, it was one of the few times we didn't tell we pulled the prank.

My good friend and closest rival all those school years was Clara Lambie. She was smart, clever, and strong willed. She and I cheered together in junior high, and both of us liked to be the center of attention. Her mother, Jesse, was one of my favorite moms. Jesse taught me how to play canasta, laughed at Clara and me for being silly, and was an excellent seamstress. Clara's mom and dad took us all over southern West Virginia to attend sporting activities, and always treated me special. Now Clara had one teacher she just butted heads with—our Home Economics teacher. Clara was always in trouble with her and the Home Ec teacher's substitute. One day Clara had had enough because the substitute teacher wouldn't excuse her to go to the bathroom. The Home Economics room had sewing machines, kitchen equipment, and a back room. Clara got the cooking pot the substitute planned to use to warm up her hot chocolate, went in the back room, peed in the pot, poured it out in the sink, and then put the pot back in its place. Within a few minutes, the substitute made her pot of hot chocolate and even asked if anyone wanted to share it with her. Of course we all said, "No thank you." As with most junior high humor, we all thought it was hilarious, and to our knowledge, neither the teacher nor the substitute ever found out. As the years progressed, Clara became a top-notch teacher and was a well-respected West Virginia educator for her entire professional career! Clara Lambie bought her first car—a green, two-door Pontiac Lemans—from Daddy when she began her first-year teaching job at Welch High School.

CHAPTER 42

Big Events, Amazing Results

Big events were on the horizon at this time in my life. In March 1961, Daddy was invited to Vermont as a surprise to honor an old friend. Would you believe George Branch, alias, "Georgie Pine"? Mother didn't want to go, so he asked me to come. Our principal said I could go if all my teachers signed a paper giving permission. Of course, they did. Who wouldn't let someone fly to Vermont, then on to New York City for the St. Patrick's Day Parade and shopping? I was fourteen years old, and it was my first plane trip. After all those times I wanted to fly on a plane from Bluefield airport, Daddy and I left early one morning changing in Roanoke and then on to Binghamton, NY. We were picked up and driven to Vermont on a cold, snowy day. That was the first time I ever ate chips and dip. Who knew? After our Vermont trip, we flew directly to New York City and did our thing. At Macy's, I saw a whole floor dedicated to just shoes! I purchased a "Jackie Kennedy" straight-lined dress and a pale purple coat, along with a pillbox hat—my Easter outfit that year. It was something! I ate my first lobster at Paddy's Clam House, and there I saw a colored woman and a white man eating together. I guess I stared at them a lot, and I asked Daddy if that was OK. Daddy said,

"Sometimes in big cities people don't care about that kind of thing." We went to NBC studios to see the game show *Concentration* with Hugh Downs and later in the evening to see *The Tonight Show* with Jack Paar, pre-Johnny Carson. Both TV programs were live. The noise, bright lights, traffic, and hustle-bustle of the city were just what I imagined.

As ninth graders, we had our first prom. My date was Jimmy C., and Mom and I shopped at Nelson's Ladies Shop in Princeton, "Foremost in Style," to buy my dress. We purchased a pale-green, tea-length, net and tulle dress that cost $27.99, matching tinted shoes at $10.99, my first strapless bra for $5.95, and gloves for $2. The total with tax was $48.33. That was big money. I only remember being chilly in that big gymnasium, having my first corsage, and dancing a lot. My strapless bra kept slipping since I had nothing to fill it out. I considered Jimmy C. my boyfriend, and he gave me a yellow, heart-shaped box of candy for Valentine's Day too. I had liked him on and off since the sixth grade.

Most special of all was our next big ninth-grade event, the National Junior Honor Society Mother–Daughter Tea held in mid-May. I dressed up in a very fancy dress, gloves, and my Jackie Kennedy pillbox hat. The most special part was that Mother and Remmie attended. Mother had her black-and-white, polka-dot, two-piece dress, gloves, and wide-brimmed hat. Remmie wore a nice, navy-blue dress, elbow-length gloves, and a white, wide-brimmed hat. Remmie looked beautiful, and Mother was the best-dressed and youngest-looking mother there.

Another big event for Judy and me centered around our fourteenth birthdays—hers in November and mine in December. She waited for my birthday, and then the two of us went to the post office and asked Mamie, the postmistress, for Social Security applications. Unlike today when Social Security numbers are issued at birth, getting your Social Security card was a rite of passage. Of course, Mamie quizzed us to be sure we were of age. We filled out our applications in our best handwriting and turned them back in to Mamie. We hung around the post office for days, waiting for them to come back from Washington, DC. When they finally arrived, Mamie was sure to say, "Jenna Lou, your Social Security card came in." We once again wrote our signatures in our best handwriting, and proudly carried them in our billfolds along with our friends' school pictures. I still have my original card; I bet Judy does too.

A lesser event was the science project from hell. Remember, science and math had become the priority in America during the Cold War. We had to beat the Russians in space! I hated the whole science-project thing. One of our trend-setting classmates in the ninth grade, who was pretty and smart, told some of the girls she had her first car date when she was in the fifth grade. However, we didn't realize she was such an electrical engineer. We soon found out when the science projects came due. As I remember, she had taken a wooden cabinet from an old television set, took out all the components, and installed a motor that attached to her solar system. The planets were proportional in relation to the sun, and rotated accordingly. It was fantastic! She won the E-N Junior High Science Fair and went on to several other competitions. Since all the rest of us had help from our parents in our feeble attempts, her mastery of engineering was overwhelming. Someone said her dad had mechanical ability, so maybe she just inherited all that skill. Who knows?

Chapter 43

Young At Heart

The travel bug continued when our ninth-grade class and some of the eighth graders went on a trip to Colonial Williamsburg. It was special because we all wore dresses we made in Home Economics on that trip! That year we spent our first night in a hotel in Richmond—no more sleeping in the bus' upper-luggage racks for me like last year. Our first stop was in Natural Bridge, the place where Mother and Daddy spent their honeymoon. Our itinerary included Charlottesville, Monticello, and Richmond. We were hot stuff staying at the Hotel King Carter at Eighth and Broad Street. I roomed with Judy, Janet Glass, and Linda Jones. I am sure we stayed up most of the night talking or worrying about a hotel fire. The next morning we ate again at the bus station, toured Richmond, got a boxed lunch from the bus station, and then departed for Williamsburg. We were impressed, and had a lot of fun taking pictures of each of us in the old-time stockade. We also went to Jamestown. I don't think all of the history really sunk in, but years later when I lived in Yorktown, I loved being in Williamsburg in the fall, having my Christmas cards done at the Olde Print Shop, and eating at the taverns on special occasions.

Most of our teachers were young—in their twenties—and had lots of new, young ideas. The leaders of that energetic faculty included Mary Thomason, Patty Boyd, Shirley Miller, Emily Keyser, Jack Byrd, Bill Bohon, and Frank Marino. Under these go-getter faculty members, the school sponsored many activities and moneymaking events such as dances, parties, sock hops, and auctions. Students had to write a letter to an important person and ask for an article to auction. Classmates received photos from movie stars and trinkets from local celebrities, including a badge from *Dragnet* and a photo of Peter Lawford. Of course I wrote to Jackie Kennedy for my request. The White House sent an engraved card, with a photo of the White House and her signature. It came with a letter from Letitia Baldrige, which said among other polite words, "She sends her very best wishes for the success of your benefit." I made Mother promise I could get the bid for that article when it came up for auction. It was touch and go but I got it for twelve dollars, one of the more expensive items. Was I ever happy!

Another must-have for me was a vendor's sample bracelet with charms that spelled out "Elkhorn Northfork" in white and blue, our school colors. Once again, I begged and begged for Mother to bid on the bracelet. She must have been in a good mood that night because I ended up getting the bracelet, which I still have. The big steal of the evening was the *Dragnet* badge. We bid and got that for three dollars. While I have had the badge since 1961, I never really paid any attention to it. Fifty years later, in November 2011, I was watching *Pawn Stars*, one of my favorite shows. A lady brought the exact badge to the show. She said her uncle worked on the show and gave her a replica of the badge, which was really rare. Would you believe they gave her $350 for that badge? Thanks Mom!

We had one very strict, well-respected, popular teacher, Mr. Russell. (Mr. Russell also helped his father run the Starland Drive-In Theatre during the summers.) A tall, handsome man and an innovative teacher, he was the first teacher I ever knew to use an overhead projector in the classroom. Mr. Russell taught math, including Algebra I. He would use his overhead projector instead of writing on the chalkboard, and it was fun watching him use the writing pens to do algebra problems. During that time, student confidentiality was not an issue. As such, Mr. Russell had five boards—one for each of his classes—attached high on the wall in the back of the room that listed all students' names and grade-point averages. At any given time, we all knew everyone else's average. Students who were good in math didn't seem to have a problem with this whole process, while those with lower averages had very bruised egos. To further accentuate the importance of grade-point averages and to motivate all of us to achieve our best, at the end of each nine weeks, Mr. Russell reseated everyone according to their average. The student with the highest grade-point average was seated at the best spot in the room. The top student in our Algebra I class, usually Jane Clark, got to be in the first seat right by his desk. That would begin "A" row. Then the rest would follow row by row until you got to the lowest average in the room. I started out at the back of "B" row, but by the end of the first semester, ended up in the middle of "D" row. This was hard for me, as I was used to sitting up front in every class, and did well in all my classes except this one. We never thought about getting a tutor to help me with algebra, but Mother religiously met with Mr. Russell every nine weeks concerned about my grade-point average. Consequently, I ended up with a D for my overall first-semester grade. I always said I wasn't good in math, but that still didn't keep me out of hot water for that one.

Ninth-grade graduation was exciting! We were on our way to high school! We even had a graduation ceremony with caps and gowns. Although I had mostly A's in all my classes and was one of the top-ranked students, that D in Algebra I proved to be a major problem for me. A county rule from the Board of Education dictated that any student with a D as a semester grade could not receive special recognition, no matter how high their overall grade-point average. That meant I could not be on the ninth-grade graduation program and give a speech. That also meant major hot water from home. So in order to get my name on the graduation program and to keep Mother happy, I needed a plan. The plan was this: I volunteered to sing for graduation. I sang "Young at Heart," the song made popular by Frank Sinatra. I chose that one simply because we had the sheet music in the piano bench from Martha's piano lessons. I did pull it off, but never sang solo in public again. Woodrow Helms told Daddy he knew I would somehow figure out how to steal the show. Interestingly, when a good friend of both us girls, Kenneth Roberts, became superintendent of McDowell County Schools years later, he changed that "no-D rule." He told me he remembered my whole situation and didn't think it was fair. Kenneth's first car was an eye-popping, gorgeous, gold GTO convertible he purchased from Daddy when he began his teaching career in McDowell County.

CHAPTER 44

Dancing in the Streets

Street dances were a big thing in the early 1960s. A local DJ from WELC or WOVE in Welch would show up at Daddy's dealership or at Carroll's. The car lots were cleared, ropes were put up around the lot, and a small fee would be charged. All the teenagers flocked to the lots and danced. These events were sponsored by a local ladies club or civic group. Most of the townsfolk would gather around and watch. Sometimes the dances would be held after special events such as Homecoming or Back-to-School night. These dances were held throughout a three-year period, but it seemed like we had most during my freshman and sophomore years. At first no colored kids ever showed up, but as time passed, the colored kids would gather near the end of the lot and boogie around outside the ropes. They were never allowed to come in. The local and state police would shoo them away. After integration was taken seriously, the City of Northfork stopped the street dances. Northfork Mayor Cecil Moore decided it was easier to ban the dances than to let the white kids dance with the coloreds.

Now this Cecil was a character. He had a dynamic personality, and was always in trouble with his wife due to his escapades. He got in so much trouble one time, his wife moved out while Cecil was on a "business" trip. To make a point, not only did she take everything, but she also took the kitchen sink! It took many months, but he did sweet talk his way back. Cecil did buy many cars from Daddy.

Chapter 45

Don't Talk to Strangers

Our family just didn't seem to get religion right. Daddy was a non-practicing Catholic, Mother was a Presbyterian; Martha and I went to the Northfork Baptist Church. A new priest came in the area during my ninth-grade year. Daddy sold him a car, and I became Catholic. I was never sure if Daddy threw my soul in along with the floor mats, but Daddy started going to mass. The priest, Father Ryan, was wonderful. He started a youth club and let us dance in the church basement—no way the Baptists would do that! Plus, all the cute boys I liked were Catholic. More seriously, I needed the stability Catholicism offered me, and I had great role models at church, namely Sue Arena, Mary Morello, Nannie Giardina, Nellie Constantino, and Rose Romeo. I took instructions and was baptized in August just before entering the tenth grade. It was on a Saturday. Daddy, Martha, Nonna, Uncle Jimmy, and Aunt Lora Mae were among those who attended my ceremony. Mother didn't believe in Catholicism or Catholics so she didn't go. She said, "Catholics pray to statutes." I wanted to go to the movies that Saturday, but Mother wouldn't let me go because I had just been baptized. More of Mother's logic. I did take my First Communion on Sunday in front of the whole church and had to wear white—a strict social rule, even though I was a teenager at the time. I loved being Catholic. Remember Jackie Kennedy was Catholic!

Between my ninth-and tenth-grade years, Mother and Daddy permitted me to visit Aunt Gladys and Uncle Bill, traveling on the bus all by myself. I think I wrote my own ticket for the eight-hour trip. I left from Bluefield on Greyhound, through Charleston and on to Wheeling, changing buses and then heading towards Pittsburgh with my stop in Little Washington. Having ridden the bus many times and being the bus expert that I was, I didn't give it a thought. Personal safety wasn't an issue either since Mother told me to sit near the bus driver, which I did. Still, I felt very grown up!

Aunt Gladys and Uncle Bill lived in a big, three-story Victorian house. They lived on the first floor and rented out the second and third floors as apartments. The house was located at the corner of Jefferson and Henderson Avenues. An Amoco gas station was dug out from the basement. Uncle Bill ran the station, along with his boat sales. He only had to walk down the basement steps, walk a few feet further, and he would be at work inside the gas station. The Sunoco station across the street and Uncle Bill's Amoco were always having gas wars. I remember seeing the gas price on those metal stands by the gas pumps reading nine and a half cents a gallon. Uncle Bill's German Shepherd, Major, ran loose at night inside the gas station, guarding the business. Major was so well trained he could even stomp out a cigarette butt with his big paw.

During my visit I shopped, went to the beauty shop, and watched a lot of Pittsburgh TV. On the way home, I talked to some college students, even though Mother told me not to talk to strangers. Their big news concerned the new zip code system for the mail. I knew Mamie at the post office had to be excited since Northfork would now be known as 24868! I thought I was hot stuff when I could converse with Mamie about the new system. I said, "Hey, Mamie, when do we start our new zip code? What happens if you don't have a zip code on the letter? Will we still be confused with Norfolk, Virginia?"

Not just zip codes, but more new changes entered our lives. About that time, we also got normal telephone numbers—396B, a party line no longer—with an area code and seven numbers. More exciting for me was our new garbage system—no more throwing trash in the creek. The garbagemen came once a week, picked it up, and hauled it off. Guess what? Kroger in Northfork got modern, new cash registers and an automatic belt at the check-out stations that moved groceries quickly. Modern times were "terrific," as the Kennedys would say.

While I was traveling and learning new prayers that summer, three of our tenth-grade friends would become the "It" girls the moment school started. The Northfork–Elkhorn High School Band was the focal point of the school's social system. Becoming a majorette was a signal a girl had made it in Northfork. To that point, girls could not become a majorette until their junior year. Well that changed when Joddy Crouch, Sandra Cannady, and Beatrice Caudill were chosen to be majorettes as sophomores. That was instant popularity, and word got around before school started that the class of 1964 was on its way!

We just couldn't wait until August 29, 1961 to start high school. No more riding the bus up Rt. 52 to the junior high; we could walk, and usually did from school. But in the morning, after Daddy fixed my breakfast, he drove me to school on his way to work. As with Martha, the first stop of the day was at the local teen joint, Mahaffeys. Martha's routine was to give Daddy a kiss on the cheek and hop out. One morning when the car stopped, out of habit, Martha gave him a fast peck on the cheek. Unfortunately, it wasn't Daddy. It was Heavy. Dad left for work early and then sent the washroom attendant, Heavy, to pick Martha up. His name pretty much described him. He was big, strong, and very colored. Both

Heavy and Martha were beyond humiliation! Learning another lesson from Martha, I was sure to never make that mistake when Daddy sent Heavy to pick me up for school.

Chapter 46

Teen Heaven: Mahaffeys

High school and the tenth grade made us feel like sophomore big dogs. Shelia, Judy, Mary, and I got THE BOOTH at Mahaffeys beside the long window seat near the juniors, excited to take our places the very first day of school! Mahaffeys, located directly on Rt. 52, had been the place for kids since the 1940s. Northfork–Elkhorn High School was on one side of Mahaffeys, and the Northfork Baptist Church was on the other side. One wall displayed photos of local World War II servicemen, and another showcased all the Kentucky Derby winners since Whirlaway in 1941. The décor was originally orange and black for the old Northfork High School Big Orange colors. The chrome-edged tables and booths that lined the inner walls were black with orange, trim piping on the booths. Four double, French doors lined the side of the longest wall, but most everyone entered through the side door. As you came through that door, you came face-to-face with Pop Mahaffey, who sat in his rocker, checking out everyone who entered. Over Pop's left shoulder were two bathrooms, with the girls' room being the busiest.

The girls' bathroom was only big enough for a commode, a basin wedged against the wall, and a mirror over the sink. The door swung open to the right and would block the entire window when any girl entered. To describe it as small was an exaggeration, but that did not mean seven or eight girls couldn't squeeze into that space. Sometimes the cigarette smoke hung so thick and the smell so strong, you could hardly breathe. Pop would call out, "You girls smoking?" A girl nearest the door would open it up just a peek, yelling, "No, Pop, we aren't. We don't smoke." Leaving wasn't easy since the girls had to first open the little window to let the smoke escape, and everyone had to wave their arms and hands to move the smoke out.

Inside was a wooden dance floor with a jukebox taking the most prominent spot. Pop got the newest and best music maker every year, but we especially loved when Pop updated the records in the jukebox—a big dot deal to us kids. We pumped in ten cents a record; a quarter gave you three records in a row. A long soda counter and fountain ran behind the jukebox. Pop had a public telephone booth on site, and it was always busy with some boy sweet-talking a girl or some gal talking to a not-so-welcome-at-home boyfriend. This was Northfork's hangout, and even the kids from Welch knew not to come uninvited. Until she died in the early 1960s, Ma Mahaffey worked on site with her daughter, Vivian. Vivian was at least in her late forties, single, and worked the soda fountain. After Ma died, they didn't sell food but had good soda drinks, chips, candy, ice cream, and other confections. One of my best memories is Vivian personally chipping the ice for our drinks to the beat of the rock-and-roll tunes as they played on the jukebox.

The high school kids met there every morning before school. Everyone had their own tables, staked out at the beginning of the year. As the buses and cars pulled into school, everyone rushed to Mahaffeys to have a couple of dances before school started. At lunch the girls ate at Mahaffeys. Vivian would have everyone's drinks on the table when they arrived for lunch. The boys ate across the street at the Blue Moon Café, owned by the Perez family. So after the boys ate their brown-bagged lunches, some would come over, sit on the long radiator bench, and act bored. But some would ask the girls to dance. A lot of guys hung around the jukebox, and a lot of girls danced to the rock-and-roll music with other gals.

The guys who didn't come inside would stroll across the highway from the Blue Moon and gather on the steps in front of the double doors at Mahaffeys. Each guy would light up, puff on his cigarette, and blow perfect smoke rings into the air. There they stood, waiting for the girls to come rushing by on their way into Mahaffeys. The guys would puff harder, blowing more smoke rings, and eyeing the girls. They just loitered around, waiting for the girls to return, and rushed back to class after lunch. The only other place in town where you might see guys standing along the roadways was at the intersection of Crumpler Road and Route 52, right beside Angelo's store. This spot was right before the vehicles gathered up speed to pull Kyle Hill, so it was the perfect location for the guys to catch a ride up the road. All they had to do was stick out their thumb, maybe wave a hand or give a whistle, and someone would stop to give them a ride. We never saw a girl or woman hitching a ride, and hitchhiking was never considered a safety issue.

During Martha's era, the couples who didn't dance at Mahaffeys during lunch would sit on the steps of the Northfork Baptist Church—the perfect place to make out. Trouble was the church steps were in plain sight of the highway. Town gossip took over, and a few reputations were tarnished. During my era the couples got smart and moved to the back side of the high school near the fire escape, out of sight. Only occasionally did the principal or a teacher patrol that area. After school, kids who did not ride the bus rushed back to Mahaffeys and danced for a half hour before heading home.

Sometimes Pop Mahaffey would schedule a private birthday or Sub Deb party, decorating with crepe paper in special colors. It was a BIG deal! Mahaffeys also opened before and after football and basketball games, before and after summer band practice, and Friday and Saturday nights. However, Pop closed the first two weeks of May so he, Ma, and Vivian could go to the Kentucky Derby. One year we were all excited when Vivian came back from the derby with a full set of new teeth.

When any new dance came down from *American Bandstand*, such as the Stroll, Twist, or the Mashed Potato, Pop wouldn't let anyone dance them because he said they were vulgar. We just stuck to "bebop" as he called it. Every Mahaffey follower loved the place. Ma, Pop, and Vivian were fixtures for years. They knew all our families, and expected us to behave. Each school year—five days a week for 180 days—this pattern played out at Mahaffeys, year after year. This ritual at Mahaffeys was as important to us as any learning we got in the classroom. About the time that school desegregation began, Pop closed Mahaffeys, and that tradition faded into wonderful memories held dear by past generations of Northfork students. Pop drove a classic, four-door Oldsmobile model he bought from Carroll's in the early 1950s.

At Northfork–Elkhorn High School, N–E for short, we had lots of drama but no drama club. There was no formal guidance program, but we did have football, basketball, and track for the boys. There was no baseball, golf, or girls' sports. Our big activities were the N–E Marching and Concert Band, the newspaper, the yearbook, Future Teachers, choir, and a few other clubs. There were three curriculum tracts: College Prep, Commercial, and General. Some of the boys went half a day to the McDowell County Vocational School in Welch. Girls did not do that.

CHAPTER 47

Hot Shot Sophomores!

I got through high school on Martha's reputation. I decided that to make A's and keep Mother happy, I would follow the curriculum that did not include algebra or higher-level sciences. With no school guidance counselor to help kids plan school and life after high school, I decided the secretarial curriculum was best. Remember, when Martha left for college, I assumed the role of making the family look good, so the pressure was on. One B on the report card could put Mother into a frenzy. When I got a B in English and one in History, there was hell to pay. So with no career planning, life was just going to happen. What kid knew anything about planning ahead?

As the school year started, we got to meet all the kids from Keystone who came from their own junior high school. One of my new favorite friends from Keystone was Carol "Boogie" Flippen. Years before, Keystone was the largest and most populated town in McDowell County—even more so than Welch, the county seat. Two reasons accounted for Keystone's growth. First, it was the site of Eastern Coal Company's largest coal mine. Second, and the reason most discussed, was Keystone's red-light district: its houses of ill repute, known widely throughout the eastern United Stated as "Cinder Bottom."

In September, right before Martha was to go back to Concord for another year, she told Mother and Daddy she had eloped with her long-time boyfriend, who was from a very prominent family. While Daddy was conciliatory, Mother had a fit. Talk about explosions! Martha did finish college as promised, but she obviously didn't follow Mother's game plan. Of course, we never knew what Mother's game plan was anyway.

I tried out and made the cheerleading squad. Boy, was I excited! The student body population selected Connie Lambert and me to be cheerleaders for the rest of our high school life. I joined every club I could and got into the swing of being a sophomore.

Judy and I were very excited to go shopping in Bluefield with our moms that fall. Mother drove us to Lerner's where we bought some school outfits. Our very best buy was our matching coats with "faux" fur collars. We always kept the fur on those fashionable winter coats! After we shopped, we went to the lunch counter at Kresge's for a hamburger. As with Martha's age group, we still wore dresses, skirts, sweaters, and flat shoes to school. We still did not wear any type of slacks, jeans, or shorts to school. While we never had a written dress code, we knew what was expected, and at N–E High School we all conformed.

All dressed up, Remmie and Mother are ready for the Jr. Honor Society Mother–Daughter Tea.

Judy Helms and Jenna Lou all decked out in the faux fur-collared coats.
Photo courtesy of Judy Helms Sargent

Chapter 48

Qui Aime Bien, Chatie Bien

I took English, Biology, Business Math, Band, and Foreign Language that year. All were good classes except Foreign Language, which was unbearable. We didn't like our Foreign Language/English teacher, Mrs. Bresey. She lived about fifty miles away, so she stayed at a lady's house in Keystone during the week and traveled home on weekends. An older woman, this was her first year of classroom teaching. She had no classroom discipline, and I needed a teacher who was strict and could not be run over. She figured all of us cheated using our textbooks during tests, so she would take up our textbooks at test time. We went one better. We'd get the textbooks from second-period students and use these. She just didn't have a clue. One day Ronnie Louthen came in and told Mrs. Bresey that the principal needed to see her right away. When she left the room, we turned off all the lights, turned our desks around, and all pretended to be asleep. Mrs. Bresey rushed back into the classroom in a flurry and started screaming. As her false teeth slipped, she yelled, "Miss Gianato, I know that this is your fault."

I think Mrs. Bresey decided to use psychology on Judy and me. One weekend she did not go home, and invited us to her rooming house to grade papers for her. She made us some Tang—the drink of astronauts—which was funny to us because we thought Tang was a breakfast drink, another strict social rule. During that day, she was friendly with us. Afterward, we still didn't show her any respect, so nothing really changed. When term-paper time came in English, Judy and I brushed up our Kennedy papers again, updating them with a few new facts. Shelia Gravely wanted something easy to do, so she wrote a biography of Caroline Kennedy. Caroline, only five years old, didn't make for a lengthy paper, but she did have one complete chapter on Caroline and her pony, Macaroni. Of course, Judy and I had all the materials for Shelia to use.

Mrs. Bresey had a good singing voice. To get out of doing anything academic, we'd ask Mrs. Bresey to sing for us, and as she sang, her false teeth always slipped. If I got a C in conduct on my report card, I would be thrown off the cheerleading squad. So every nine weeks at report card time, I'd talk Mrs. Bresey out of giving me a C. Well, one time she gave me a B-, and of course, I was in hot water. I told Mother and Daddy that Mrs. Bresey didn't like me, and she had no discipline in her classroom. Of course Mother and Daddy felt for sure this was just an excuse on my part. One day Daddy and I were at the post office talking to Mamie, who was behind the post-office window. Mrs. Bresey came in and I said, "Mrs. Bresey, I'd like you to meet my dad, Luke Gianato." Daddy said, "I have heard a lot about you." At that point, she went into some altered state and started yelling about how miserable I made her life, how disrespectful I was, and on and on and on. Having heard all he wanted, Daddy turned away from her and said to me, "She is a damn nut." Everyone in the post office heard every word! At dinner that night I told Daddy, "I told you so!" They never said any more about my behavior in her classroom. Mrs. Bresey taught another year in McDowell County and then transferred to a nearby county. Mrs. Bresey lived to be well over one hundred! I wonder if she ever used that Tang ploy with any other students during her teaching career.

At the end of that sophomore year—trying to be a smart-aleck—I had Mrs. Bresey sign my yearbook. She wrote a French phrase that I never really had any desire to translate. But fifty years later, I googled the French phrase Mrs. Bresey had written, "Qui Aime Bien, Chatie Bien," which means "Spare the rod and spoil the child." Our mutual disrespect was quite evident, and I am certain if she did drive, she never would have bought a car from Daddy!

One popular and seasoned teacher, Mr. Scolery, was my Business Math teacher. He was handicapped and walked with crutches. Mr. Scolery did drive his Chrysler with a push-button transmission, so his hands weren't such a problem. However, he had difficulty writing on the chalkboard, so we girls all volunteered to write on the board for him. That was about all I did other than copy math answers from Judy. I sat next to Judy, and thinking I was clever, I would sneak a look at her answers during tests. Sometimes I'd just take her paper and write down the correct answer. Funny thing happened. At lunch break one day in the early 1970s, Martha—the English teacher by now—and Mr. Scolery were in the school's furnace room smoking. Mr. Scolery asked, "Whatever happened to your sister?" Martha said, "She taught business courses several years in East Liverpool, Ohio, but she is currently a business teacher in Yorktown, Virginia, teaching business math." Choking on his cigarette smoke and laughing as hard as he could, he gasped, "Well, just whose lesson plans is she copying now?"

So basically I had a range of teachers from very strict, to those who wanted to be your friend, to those who didn't have a clue. Fortunately when I taught, I knew all the tricks and could nip all those crafty kids' tricks in the bud.

CHAPTER 49

The GTO

After I converted to Catholicism during the tenth grade, I started going to Youth Club. Father Ryan was the priest for both Powhatan and Kimball's churches, so Youth Club was held in either of the churches' basements. The kids from our end of the county attended along with the ones from Kimball. Kimball kids went to Welch High School, so it was a great opportunity for us to make new friends even though our schools were rivals. There I met Jimmy Frank, who was just so cute and a good dancer. He became my boyfriend and came to our high school Christmas dance. During the Christmas holidays, the Gary Catholic Youth Club had a semiformal dance at the Gary Country Club—big stuff back then. My date was Jimmy Frank. We triple dated with my old boyfriend Jimmy C. and his date, Fostina. And then there was Frankie, Jimmy C.'s brother. Frankie was the best-looking guy in all of southern West Virginia. He dated the prettiest girls in a four-county area, and he knew them all. Frankie, who had just gotten his driver's license, agreed to go to the dance if he could drive. His mother's only condition was that he take "a good, Catholic girl." He took my friend, Antoinette Angelo. So off we all went on a cold, snowy night on those twisty, narrow roads to Gary by way of Welch, picking up Jimmy Frank in Kimball. After the dance it was still snowing hard. We took the Welch route home, going to the Sterling Drive-In, and of course our trip took forever in the snowstorm. We all lied to cover up our foolishness and to keep Frankie out of trouble. Our story—Frankie had to drive extremely slow and carefully on the slick roads. We all left out the side-trip detour to the Sterling Drive-In. So much for our Catholic Youth Club and truthfulness, but we weren't too worried because our lies were just venial sins!

Basketball season came and went, and I had my first of many experiences with Daddy calling out the referees. Our gym had a stage where all the businessmen sat. I'd be cheering along, and then I'd see Daddy hollering and jumping around, yelling to the referee about a bad call. During one game, Dad was so excited he jumped off the stage flatfooted and got in the referee's face. The kids would say, "Jenna Lou, your dad is acting up again!" After basketball came April and our Spring Band Concert, drawing a large crowd of proud parents. The month of May saw the big band competition in Bluefield. We always got the highest rating and had the longest line of majorettes and flag girls. N–E Marching Band was for sure the best in southern West Virginia.

NASCAR-racing season became big as Pontiac had cars in the races, and many of Dad's employees were die-hard fans. A few of the employees took off to Florida for the Daytona 500 each spring. GTOs were the great, new Pontiac. Several of the hip boys in Northfork drove them, driving down the road with those roaring "glass packs" on their mufflers. Major League Baseball was the other passion around the garage. Bob Norris loved the Cincinnati Reds so much he named his son Joey Jay after the Cincinnati player. All work would stop at the dealership when the All-Star Baseball game came on. A lot of bets were made, and this too became a tradition.

Chapter 50

Banko Not Bingo

Our end of the county did have a few predictable entertainment events. Every year the Thomas Joyland Carnival rolled into McDowell County. In late March, the signs would begin to show up on telephone poles, giving notice the carnival would be here in May. We all loved it. The carnival crew usually pitched the tents for the carnival in Mother's old stomping grounds, Vivian Bottom. The rides, the music, the lights, and the greasy-food smells were just exciting. The rides were our favorites, especially the Whip or the Ferris wheel, but we weren't allowed to look at the sideshows because there were too many hootchy-kootchy girls and gypsies there. Mother told me that only gypsies and old Italians had their ears pierced, and for me not to even think about it. It would be several years before I did. There was one thing about all those carnival signs hanging on the poles. No one took them down after the carnival left, so it was October before they finally blew off the telephone poles or faded out.

Another favorite was the Freeman Theatre in Northfork, which sat along Elkhorn Creek by the railroad track and next door to the Masonic Lodge. The theater had a big parking lot, which served as overflow parking during high school basketball games. If there wasn't a football or basketball game on Friday night, we went to the movies. (We always said we were going to "the movies," while the Yankee boys from New York would say "flicks," and the southern girls from Mississippi called the movies, "the picture show.") Saturday night was a definite with two movies costing forty cents for adults. Before the second movie, the house lights went up, lovers quit smooching, and the manager took center stage with a big board with numbers ready for us to play "Banko." With our numbered paper cards, the manager would call the numbers, and we could win up to five dollars for our match. Instead of winners yelling "Bingo," we yelled "Banko."

The theater had strict seating arrangements. The white folks occupied two-thirds of the theater, and the colored people had one-third. The whites had their own entrance and their own bathroom, the coloreds the same. The bathrooms always smelled, were dirty, and had water on the floors. You had to hold your breath the whole time you went to the bathroom—from the ten steps you walked down to the basement restroom until you returned back to the top. Kids mostly sat in the balcony so we could see who was making out. Our seats were usually near the divider pole that separated the whites' section from the coloreds'. A long banister ran from the balcony to the first row, marking the separation line. A lot of coloreds went to the movies and seemed to have a good time. They didn't pay any attention to us, and we paid no attention to them. We never knew why the theater was called the "Freeman," and I don't remember any coloreds ever winning Banko!

Just like the new television cable that ran down the mountain to the houses in Elkridge and opened up the world, politics in the 1950s and 1960s showed change in McDowell County. Such a change was the election of Elizabeth Drewry, the first colored woman to be elected to the West Virginia House of Delegates. A red-haired, small-framed lady who always dressed to the nines, Mrs. Drewry served from 1950-1964. She represented the Northfork district, but I never thought of her as being my representative. Then again, I never thought about that sort of thing. I do remember that Election Day was a big deal in McDowell County, especially national elections. Supposedly a lot of money changed hands. Many candidates would get a team of drivers to pick up those potential voters who didn't have a ride to the polling place and take them to vote. Some people voted more than once. We heard of some people voting, not only in Northfork and Keystone, but also in Maybeury too. While both Republican and Democratic party members were present at the polling places, the Democrat party favorites got to work the polls and made a few dollars on the side from the party—or so we were told. In later years, one polling official even told me how he would go into the voting machine, push all the levers, and then tell the next voter all they had to do was push the one switch. I don't think there was ever any worry that a Republican would be elected to any office in our little Northfork district anyway.

CHAPTER 51

Summer of 1962

My big deal during the summer before my junior year was my bus trip to Washington, DC, by myself. Sharon McCarthy's family had moved to DC during the exodus from the coalfields due to the consolidation of the coal companies. Her dad had worked briefly for Daddy, and they were well respected in the community. She and I hooked up after her cousin married a local man, and she came for the wedding. She and I hung out together and began corresponding. For my trip, I wrote my own ticket going through Roanoke, Staunton, and on up to DC. The McCarthys met me at the bus station, and I was thrilled to be in Washington, DC. Maybe I would see Jackie Kennedy! We had a ball. She fixed me up with dates, and we had our hair done "DC style" with lots of teasing and lots of hairspray. We went to Rock Springs Park, shopped, and took a tour of the White House. I was in seventh heaven! I was convinced I was meant to be in DC.

Appearances, clothes, and makeup were paramount for all of us high school girls. Hair was always a big topic, and mostly bouffant like Jackie Kennedy. I remember we spent hours and hours underneath our portable Sunbeam hair dryers. Long before blow-dryers and curling irons, we would roll our hair in brush rollers while it was wet and then put a big hood over the rollers. The hood was connected to the dryer by a long tube. We couldn't go very far while our hair was drying since the tube was not that long.

We girls spent a lot of time in G.C. Murphy's looking at lipstick and nail polish. I really wanted to wear purple, but Mother said only colored women and Arlene Blevins wore purple lipstick. No one thought anything about animal testing with beauty products or about formaldehyde in nail polish. A "vegan" would have probably been a fictional outer space character on the TV show, *The Twilight Zone*. We didn't have panty hose then, so we wore Carolina Moon stockings held up with a garter belt. Buying hose was an important purchase too. Nails were not such a big deal because we had to keep our nails short so we could hit the manual typewriter keys just perfectly.

Our entire gang was excited to be high school juniors and learn things like typing and shorthand. No more math for me! Summer band was fun, and on a lark I tried out for majorette, although I knew that I would be banner carrier/cheerleader and couldn't do all three. The big news at summer band was that Joddy Crouch was chosen as Head Drum Majorette as a junior! Another first for N–E since only seniors in the past had been given that honor. All of her friends and admirers in the class of 1964 were happy and proud for her!

Jimmy C. and I started going together again, even though I did like Jimmy Frank too. Since Jimmy Frank went to Welch High School, our contact was limited. I was officially allowed to car date when I was sixteen. A typical car date involved driving to Welch to the Sterling or West Virginia Drive-Ins, getting a hamburger, and driving home. The rest of the dates were in town at a game or the movies. Jimmy C. and I were usually too busy dancing to do much making out. While there was parking, we were supposedly "saving ourselves for marriage." Getting "pragnat" was not an option and totally out of the question—a strict social rule. Those who did get "pragnat" all got married. Some of us were still pretty naïve. We always put Charlotte Kowaleski up to asking Father Ryan questions during confession like, "Will I go to Hell for French kissing?" I don't think we cared if he answered yes, since that was the closest some of us got to sex education.

Big events, schoolwise, included my invitation to become a member of the National Honor Society. We juniors ordered our class rings, and I continued to make good grades and work on the yearbook. I loved Mrs. Byrd, my Shorthand teacher, and Miss Vecillio, my Typing teacher. When I later taught both those subjects, I would often think of them and what good role models they were for me. Cheering for football and basketball seasons was fun, and I played the flute and the piccolo for concert season. Shelia began dating Dickie Watson, Clara Lambie was still with Charlie Hamer, Linda Watson was with Bill Ford, Boogie was with Dickie Eldreth, and Joddy Crouch and Connie Lambert dated several of their other favorite guys. School and all its activities were fun, and we kids worked hard at making the fun parts of our lives exciting.

Chapter 52

Battle of the Bands

It was a brisk but sunny morning when the N–E Blue Demon Marching Band, all decked out in our red, white, and blue uniforms, assembled in the parking lot of the new Northfork Post Office. It was a big day because Northfork's new post office was being dedicated, giving our little town a modern, new post office! Everyone heard that President Kennedy was coming, and we believed any rumor related to Kennedy. Of course that was just a rumor, but I do think Senator Byrd was on hand.

All the county and local officials were there, ready to make a speech and cut the red ribbon. To our surprise, the Elkhorn High School Elks Band from the colored school was also there to play for the celebration. Litz Armbrister, our band director, told us their band was invited because the post office was a federal government building and the coloreds used the facility too. As I remember, he said it had something to do with new federal equality regulations, all of which we had paid little attention.

Our band was at least twice the size of the Elks Band, but they played with a lot of spirit. We played a very traditional John Phillip Souza march. Then they played a song like, "St. Louis Woman," and all the band members would sway in various directions dancing precision jazz-like steps as they played. It was the first time many of us experienced an integrated festivity. When it was time to convene the ceremony, both bands played the National Anthem together. It was quite a new experience playing music with the coloreds in a formal activity. During the ceremony, the bands took turns playing different preselected songs. When all the speeches and ceremony ended, and I am not sure how it happened, each band began playing different songs at the same time, sort of a "battle of the bands." I think we were surprised at the whole event and that the coloreds didn't acquiesce and quit playing. The Elks Band marched out first still performing their synchronized dance movements, and some of the white kids thought the colored kids acted "uppity." Naively thinking "they" were in our territory, many thought the coloreds should have just been glad they were invited. So from that point on, McDowell County slowly began to integrate. The schools did not integrate until 1967, three years after I graduated. In fact, Martha was teaching the year integration started.

Chapter 53

Integration of the Schools

Racial integration was a double-edged sword in our part of the world in the 1960s. Even though we played with Lucy and her brother after school and every afternoon, come Monday morning, they went to the colored school on the hill, and we went downtown to our white grade school. Our separated worlds ended in 1967 with apprehension, nervous parents, and scared school kids—both white and black. After the Civil Rights Movement, colored kids were then called black.

The plan the school board adopted for our end of the county had black and white children changing schools. All the black and white elementary students were bused to Switchback Elementary, a former white school, but with its first white principal, Woodrow Helms. All black and white junior high kids in the area were bused to the former all-black Elkhorn High School. The former white high school was the base for all high schoolers—black and white—from Landgraff to the Mercer County line, a twenty-three-mile range, as the highway goes.

The plan appeared to be a logical one, but integration was not logical for two reasons. First, parents were concerned about the length of time their kids had to be on school buses. The local black and white schools before integration were no longer the neighborhood schools they once were. Secondly, at the "new" junior high, the black kids and the black teachers resented the invasion of white kids and white teachers into their school.

Tension and mouthing came to a head one afternoon on the road in front of the junior high building where Martha was teaching eighth-grade English. Black and white boys got into name-calling between classes that led to pushing, then to fighting. Mr. Waldron, the principal, yelled over the intercom, "All male teachers report to the front road; break up that fight now!" Well, that was almost an invitation for mayhem and meanness. Anyone who had access to windows on front of the building had a front-row seat to the fight and to its quick solution.

The afternoon and night custodian was a tall, muscular, black man who was also a constable for upper McDowell County. At the principal's announcement, the constable/custodian stepped out of the furnace room and crossed the highway, took a bullhorn from his car, pinned his constable badge onto his shirt, and buckled his weapon onto his hip.

He yelled loud and clear in thirty words, "If each of you black and each of you white heathens and troublemakers don't stop, sit down, and shut your mouths, my friend on my hip would settle this fight." Immediately the fighting ceased, and a nervous calm prevailed.

As Martha told her eighth-grade, racially mixed English class on the first day of the next school year, "Everything seems scary on the first day of school, and you will have some problems, but I promise you kids, we'll get all the kinks out, and things will be OK." At that, Sylvia from the back of the room called out, "Miss Teacher, you'll never be able to get all the kinks out of my black, kinky, colored hair." At that, Martha hee-hawed, Sylvia laughed and laughed, and the class roared with laughter. Humor did work miracles.

Change came slowly with integration, but the children adjusted better than the older adults. By 1968, national events continued to emphasize racial tension in the United States. A late afternoon in early April, Martha came home from work, tired and anxious to see her daughter, Laura. Big Elizabeth, the huge, black woman who helped raise Laura, and the little one were in each other's arms, hugging each other, rocking to and fro, and sobbing loudly. Big Elizabeth had her face buried in a dishtowel, and Laura's face was red from crying. Martha, seeing this, yelled, "What on earth has happened?" Laura said, "Oh mama, mama, mama," sounding like Big Elizabeth, "somebody shot Martin Luther King!"

Chapter 54

Sweet Sixteen and Driving!

But back in the spring of 1963, all I cared about was getting my driver's license. Our high school did not have Driver's Education, so we learned from our parents. Daddy had been teaching me to drive since I was fourteen. He would let me drive home from church. That was a big deal to me. One time he let me drive to Kimball, six miles away. Daddy fell asleep while I was driving. When he woke up, and I was flying low on the one straight stretch of road, he laid the law down then! All of my friends first studied the manual to take the written test. If they passed the written test, they got their learner's permit. Daddy came home for supper one night and had a learner's permit already filled out for me, and I hadn't even taken the test. Was I ever excited! While l usually could not keep a secret, I didn't tell anybody about this. I knew I would never get my license if I did.

Every night at supper, we waited for Daddy so we could all eat together. He drilled, quizzed me, and made up scenarios about driving. He would take the manual, open to a page, and start drilling. I still think he made up questions just to confuse me so he could pontificate on the rules of the road. It did seem that these rules always involved a school bus. However, Dad did throw in some of his good stories about his road experiences. I wish I had taken the test like everyone else. It was harder getting the learner's permit from Luke Gianato than from the state of West Virginia! Even Mother would roll her eyes and say, "Enough is enough" or "Hello-Pete, I didn't know that."

Once Daddy determined I knew the manual, it was time to take the driver's test. Testing occurred every Thursday at the State Police Headquarters in Roderfield, past Welch. I got out of school early and since Daddy was busy, his general manager, Raymond Kestner drove, knowing I would drive back. Raymond had one of the worst driving records in McDowell County and an even worse reputation with the women. Raymond wrecked many of Daddy's cars, and wreaked havoc on plate-glass windows. A tail gunner with the Ninth Air Force during World War II, Raymond earned the Distinguished Flying Cross and was scared of nothing and no one. He was one hell of a salesman, smart, and had an interesting laugh. Raymond always treated Martha and me with respect even though he had quite the reputation.

Now Raymond's escapades were known area-wide. The effective car salesman, he had so many irons in the fire that he would ignore details. On such an occasion, he sold a 1957 Pontiac convertible to Tony Angelo. Now in the 1950s and 1960s, a customer could have a great deal of leeway in ordering an automobile—from color to a full array of options—unlike today's auto market. That is exactly what Tony Angelo did, ordering a black Pontiac convertible with pink top, black leather interior with the pink leather insert, and pink piping along the edges of the seats.

More than six weeks later, Tony Angelo walked into the dealership, rather annoyed, wanting to know what was taking so long for his Pontiac delivery. Opening his desk drawer to get the car's order copy, Raymond glanced down, and seconds later quickly shut the drawer again. Raymond then asked Tony, "Did you hear about that big train derailment outside of Pontiac, Michigan?" When Tony indicated he had heard something about it, Raymond proceeded to explain his pink, soft-top Pontiac was on that train being shipped, but unfortunately the car was destroyed. As such, Raymond had already confirmed with Pontiac that the convertible was in production once again. Raymond assured him the car would be in within a month. Eventually Tony seemed reassured, especially when Raymond threw in a set of black fender skirts and curb feelers.

As soon as Tony left the dealership, Raymond immediately called Pontiac and verbally ordered the car, with paperwork sent at the same time. Tony's Pontiac convertible was a knockout—something really special—but he never realized Raymond forgot to place the initial order. Raymond, however, caught the wrath of Daddy's temper and large vocabulary of every known curse word in the English language. He waved his arms and gritted his teeth, throwing in his favorite expression when angry at an employee, "All you care about is quittin' time and payday!" Daddy, however, knew full well that another crisis would rear its ugly head as long as Raymond sold cars.

So on the day of my driver's test, Raymond drove like a bat out of hell to get us to Roderfield in record time. Anxious to take the test, we took Mother's smaller Tempest Convertible, thinking it would be easier to parallel park.

After the State Trooper and I drove up Premier Mountain and back, he asked me to just pull straight in and stop. I thought for sure I had failed the driving part since he didn't even let me try to parallel park. Everyone knew I left school early, and if my name was not in the *Welch Daily News*, everyone would know I failed the exam. I was surprised and relieved when Raymond came back with my driver's license. He said he told the State Trooper it wasn't necessary for me to parallel park because he had taught me everything I knew about driving. Who knows what was really said! Raymond let me drive back to Northfork and told me "to open it up" on that one straight stretch of road. I did!

Mother got a new car every year. She loved convertibles. If she put 700 miles on the car, it was a big year. I drove her car, and then later I took cars to college. I used to say that when I filled up the ashtray of one car, I got a new one. While that may be a bit of an exaggeration, it was close to true. You name it, I drove it. I especially liked the two-seater 1969 Sport Opel. It was just like the car Maxwell Smart drove on the comedy, *Get Smart*. When I had to start making car payments at the age of forty, I truly understood how fortunate I had been all those years.

CHAPTER 55

Special People, Special Times

After I joined the Catholic Church, I sang in the choir—a group with a good mixture of young girls and older ladies. One of my favorites was Rose Varelli. While I was in the choir, she became engaged to Joe Romeo. These two made a terrific-looking couple, and she was madly in love. Her wedding was just superb, she looked beautiful, and the reception was first class. My goal was to have just that perfect of a wedding. Another favorite in the choir was Rosa Lee Colo. She was two years younger than I, and she not only played the piano but also the organ. My old telephone party-line partner, Nancy Totsi, who made everyone laugh all the time, was high on my list too. I was so proud to be a choir member, especially during Christmas or Easter services. Every Monday night we had catechism, and two weeks every summer the nuns came for vacation catechism. Father Ryan taught the high schoolers, so we felt special.

During my ninth-and tenth-grade years, I sent off for girl's boarding school information. I wanted to be like Jackie Kennedy and go to boarding school. Mother would just roll her eyes and say, "You are too immature." During my junior year, I began sending off for college catalogues.

I sent requests to the University of Hawaii, Virginia Intermont (a women's college), University of Miami, George Washington University, and Howard University. It was obvious why I sent for Hawaii and Miami, but I also loved Washington, DC, so I sent for information from the two universities there. I would get all excited when Mamie at the post office would tell me I got a catalog and then hand it to me. When I got the catalog from Howard—the colored university—Daddy yelled at me, "Are you crazy? I can't believe they would send anyone whose name ends in a vowel a catalog!" I said, "Why, it is in Washington, DC?" He yelled again, "It is a colored school, and they probably thought it was a joke." I didn't know. Mamie at the post office probably got a good laugh.

I finally applied to a two-year women's college, Virginia Intermont in Bristol, Virginia. I was admitted to college before the end of my junior year, even before I took the SAT. We never even visited the campus. I just knew I wanted to go to Virginia Intermont and "get some culture." Most importantly, Mother thought it was a high-class place. By choosing it, I didn't have to go through all the hassle Martha did to please Mother about my college choice.

Throughout our high school years, we girls had several pajama parties. Shelia Gravely and Boogie Flippen had the most memorable ones. At Boogie's, her mother had one rule: No boys and no boys in cars stopping by. We followed the rules, but those boys drove by many, many times. I think we all had a puff on a cigarette, put vanilla in our Cokes because someone said we would get high, ate junk food, and gossiped. The epitome of our social standing in the fall of each year was an invitation from the Crumpler girls to us Northfork girls to spend Halloween night at their slumber party. All of us invitees rode the Crumpler bus from school with our hostesses. We ran the streets of Crumpler, watching the boys turn over the outhouses, and dressed up in some modified, cool, teenager outfit. Mostly we hung out and had a big time. I am pretty sure the Crumpler Halloween tradition began during Martha's high school tenure.

One of my favorite people was Mrs. Watson from Crumpler. Her daughter, Linda, was a friend, and Shelia dated her son, Dickie. The Watsons had the only brick house in Crumpler, and a concrete swimming pool with no filter. They had to change their water like we did. Anyone under the age of thirty-five admired Mrs. Watson's fashionable dress, makeup, and demeanor; all the jealous old biddies didn't. Thank goodness we had someone who kept up with the times. Mrs. Watson drove a two-door, blue and white Cadillac (like the one Don Draper had in *Mad Men*) she bought from Carroll's.

Top on my list of special people was Nellie Constantino. In fact, I loved that entire, big family. Nellie worked at G.C. Murphy's and could talk to me, work the cash register, answer the phone, answer customer questions, and dog out the manager all at the same time. I think I was as special to her as she was to me. We had lots of talks, and I did confide to her quite a bit about my thoughts, my worries, my ambitions, my family, and all the concerns of a teenage girl. Looking back, Nellie gave up so much for herself so her boys could buy their girlfriends expensive birthday and Christmas presents, Valentine candy, flowers for every big dance, gas money for the black-and-white 1957 Ford, and money for dates. Nellie was an excellent cook. The first lasagna I ever ate was hers, and it is still my benchmark for lasagna. Her two signature dishes were banana cake and cream puffs. Those smells always bring back Nellie to me.

Chapter 56

Noted Republican

A highlight for us each fall was the showing of the new car models. Daddy would put heavy brown paper to cover all the showroom windows to hide the new models as they came from Michigan. It helped to build the suspense. On a designated day, all the window paper came down, and General Motors had all their product lines "show" their new cars for the year. People would pour into Dad's dealership and at Carroll's Motor Sales. The dealers would have drawings and giveaways. We had key rings, ashtrays, cup holders, coffee cups, combs, window scrapers, rain bonnets, and matches, all with a message that usually said: GIANATO PONTIAC, INC., AT STOP LIGHT, NORTHFORK, 862-4255.

Car shows were big too. At one time, there were thirteen car dealerships in McDowell County. Sponsored by the McDowell County Dealers Association, all the county dealers would take a couple of cars to the armory in Welch for the event. I worked the shows, giving out brochures and trinkets. I had to dress nicely and act properly. One evening I wanted to go to the Sterling Drive-In just up the road. The car I drove to Welch was blocked in, so Reba Carroll told me I could take her

Cadillac since her car was easily available. Well, Reba's Cadillac was long and wide, as opposed to Mother's little Tempest, which I usually drove. Not having a lot of experience at driving around the speaker poles in drive-ins, I pulled into the stall of the drive-in very, very close to the left pole. I knew if I scratched up Reba's car, I would be the talk of the town. So I finally got some guy to pull it out for me. That was a close one, and I knew I would be in very hot water if I made us look bad. Reba would have had some extra mileage talking about us if Daddy had to repair that big Cadillac at his Pontiac dealership!

Always on the alert for making a few dollars more, Daddy made some extra money by cashing the "script" from Paul Miller's coal mines. Miners got paid in script, rather than in cash, which profits the owner of the company. For instance, if a miner had a $200 script paycheck, Daddy would cash his script check and give him $175. Daddy and Paul would split the $25 difference. It was all legal, and a lot of miners cashed their checks at the dealership. Even though Paul Miller and Daddy were in the script business together, Paul bought top-of-the-line Cadillacs from Carroll's.

It is hard to believe that Martha and I lived in an era where some people still could not read or write. Sometimes someone who was illiterate would buy a car, and to make the deal legal, they would have to sign their "X" instead of their signature. The "X" had to be witnessed. I was working at the dealership on one such occasion, and Daddy asked me to witness the signing of the "X." Afterward, I was being my smart, big-mouth self and made some remark about the dumb person who couldn't even write his name. Not only did I get an in-depth, long, tongue lashing and the car taken away for a week, Daddy flatly told me, "Not everyone has had the advantage of an education like you; in fact, many of these hardworking people are very smart and more creative than half the dumb-ass people I know who graduated high school. I never want to hear you belittle anyone because you think you are better than they are."

One day I was walking from town and Buster Beaman, who was seventeen at the time, came up to me and asked, "Jenna Lou, is your dad a noted Republican?" I said, "No, Buster, he is a Democrat." He then went on to tell me the army told him to get his induction papers signed by a "Noted Republican," a local businessman. I directed him to W.S. Kirkpatrick, who was a Notary Public. The next time I saw Buster, he was in his army uniform.

Chapter 57

Uncle Junior and the FBI

It had been some time since we heard from Uncle Junior. After the money episode, he laid low. He called every once in a while just to say hello. One summer afternoon, Mother got a call. It was the FBI, and they wanted to talk to her about her brother. She told me she would not invite the FBI into the house, and when they arrived, I was to have them sit on the glider in front of the swimming pool. She told me NOT TO SAY ANYTHING, but I could listen and watch.

The two men came in a black, four-door Ford and showed their FBI identification badges. As Mother instructed, I asked them to be seated on the glider. Mother also had Cokes on ice for them, which I politely distributed. One of the agents asked her, "When was the last time you heard from your brother?" Even though she had recently heard from Junior, she answered with a flick of her cigarette, "I really don't remember but probably about eight months ago." They kept asking and writing notes, and I was fascinated. Mother asked them why they wanted to know about Junior. They said something about bounced checks. When it appeared the interview was about over since Mother knew absolutely nothing, I jumped in. I started asking them how I could get a job with the FBI in Washington, DC. They promptly left, and that was the end of that.

Chapter 58

We Rule the School

One of our favorite pastimes—before e-mail, texting, or Facebook—was to write letters. Better still, we liked receiving letters. I had quite a few pen pals, and loved to go to G.C. Murphy's for new parchment stationary, along with a Sheaffer cartridge fountain pen. I particularly liked the green and dark-blue colors for my ink cartridge. The point on the pen was sharp, just like the ones used in the old days. We were able to find foreign pen pals through Judy's cousin, who was stationed in England with the air force. I loved it when Post Office Mamie, who never bought a car from Daddy, told me I had a letter from overseas. Many of our friends wrote to the guys in the army, navy, or marines, and proudly talked about places like Turkey, Germany, or Korea. Now Helen Szichok from Eureka—pronounced "Your-re-kee"—Holler had pen pals too. She wrote to the boys up at the Moundsville Prison. In fact, I remember she told us one of her favorites had two more years before he was to be released, and that he was coming to see her when he got out!

Junior/Senior prom was fun. It was the juniors' job to decorate the gym for the prom, and I remember we all spent hours making three thousand paper roses to complete our prom theme of "Moonlight and

Roses." I bought a white, strapless gown with blue netting. I dyed my hair black and had it teased high, wanting to look more Italian. We all just loved dressing up in those formals! That summer I continued to work at Dad's, filled in at the bus station, and had fun with the gang at summer band practice. Everyone kept looking forward to our senior year. Imagine! The class of 1964!

Before school began, the N–E Band took a fun trip to Daytona Beach, Florida. Band members paid for the trip themselves, but also helped raise money so all the members could go. Our band director, Litz Armbrister, was originally a Crumpler boy and had graduated from Northfork High School. He was no doubt the best bandmaster in the state. He believed that all his students should have exposure to the real world and see how it was to live in an environment outside the coalfields. Many of our classmates had not traveled far from home, and this trip was good incentive for a student to join the band. Because of trips such as this and our other band activities, our school had the largest marching and concert band in McDowell County, including more than half of our student body. Judy, Mary, Rose Kosa, and I had a fun time rooming together in Florida. Even the bus trip both ways was a hoot. Years have erased the details, but all did go without a hitch.

Senior year 1963-1964 was truly perfect—from cheerleading and being co-editor of the school yearbook, to fun classes, Mahaffey's every day, and Homecoming. The City of Northfork put on a big Homecoming Parade prior to the football game. Connie Lambert and I, as co-head cheerleaders, rode in one of Daddy's new Pontiac convertibles. We sat on top of the back seat, smiling and waving our red and blue pom-poms to the crowd lining Main Street. Mother and Daddy bought us corsages made of red and blue carnations, and we threw penny candy to the crowd and acted important. The rest of the cheer squad rode in another convertible behind us. Intertwined with Homecoming was the issue of the scoreboard dedication.

As co-editors, Joddy Crouch and I had the yearbook going full blast. Not long before Homecoming night, Mr. Atkinson, the principal, called over the school loud speaker for Joddy and me to come to his office. We had no idea what he wanted, but since the entire school knew we were going to his office, we knew it was important. Sitting behind his desk, he asked us to be seated. I knew it was something big when he began slowly in his squeaky, nasal voice, "Jen-na Lo-u-u and Jo-ddy, I have called you here since you are the yearbook editors. Even though this breaks tradition, the yearbook this year will not be dedicated to the teacher your yearbook staff has already selected." Totally surprised, I almost shouted, "Why not?" A little more than aggravated and getting red in the face, he emphatically said, carefully spacing out his words, "This year the yearbook will be dedicated to Reba Carroll, for her generosity in buying the scoreboard for the football field." I sat there shocked, stunned, and very angry. Joddy, of course, was more composed. Like the lady she was, she continued to listen as he gave further details. Knowing that I had better keep my mouth shut as we both left his office, I glared at him and was hopping mad. Imagine, the yearbook was going to be dedicated to Daddy's biggest competitor—and I was the co-editor. I was mortified.

So during halftime of the Homecoming game, Mrs. Carroll—wearing her elegant black suit, fur piece, stylish hat, and surrounded by her employees at midfield—was recognized and honored. She received earnest gratitude from both the school and the community, which actually was well deserved. The yearbook staff did place a dedication photo of the ceremony in the yearbook. From this I learned that any tradition—no matter how special or engrained in our life—can be changed or tweaked to fit any situation. Again, I wanted to question the whole situation, but Daddy told me to "put on lid on it."

CHAPTER 59

My Third President–Mr. Johnson

It has been said that the 1963-64 N–E Blue Demon football team was the best in the school's history. Under the direction of John Brant and Jennings Boyd, Northfork–Elkhorn had a winning football team that went on to the Class A State Football Tournament. The whole town got involved with a bonfire, the first ever, and four chartered buses to Logan for the tournament with Winfield. Linda Piconi joined the cheering squad as the new mascot, and wore a red demon outfit with a pitchfork, which added to all the excitement. On game day, the four buses and many cars made the trip to Logan on those crooked, two-lane roads. Full of enthusiasm, we all felt so important for being part of something special. The Northfork area was so proud of our team even though the Generals won 25–13. As a reward though, the school scheduled an Almost-Victory Dance in the school auditorium to celebrate the great season.

On that Friday afternoon, November 22, Marsha Tolliver walked down to G.C. Murphy's to buy another supply of crepe paper to finish up the decorations for the dance. Minutes later, she came back into the auditorium, quite upset, telling us she heard that President Kennedy had been shot and killed while on a campaign trip in Dallas. No official announcement was made, but news spread like wildfire. Running up to the school's third floor, I told the news to Mr. Trechock, our Government teacher, and his student teacher, our friend Tony Mack Larkin. Then I ran down to the second floor to the grade school to tell Mr. Helms. Both men loved politics and Kennedy, and were visibly upset. Everyone was.

The dance was still a go, but most didn't attend. Everyone—young and old—stayed glued to the television all weekend, like most of the nation. Mass that Sunday is still fresh in my mind, sad, but comforting. Later that morning, Mother told me she had seen on TV that Oswald had been shot. I wanted to go to the Capitol to see the President's coffin, but Mother said, "No, there is too much traffic." Strangely enough, as much as Judy and I loved the Kennedys, she and I didn't talk about the assassination very much. As young as we were then, it seemed we both knew it was the end of that era, and things would never be the same.

Eleven days before President Kennedy's assassination, Vice President Lyndon Johnson represented President Kennedy at the Veterans Day celebration and parade in Welch. The vice president was actually the substitute speaker and substitute guest of honor for the event—a stand-in for the president, who had promised to return to McDowell County for its support in the 1960 primary. Instead he sent Johnson, who flew via helicopter from Charleston, West Virginia, on that November morning. Marching in front of the Northfork–Elkhorn band carrying the school banner, I could easily see Vice President Johnson standing tall on the reviewing stand.

Following the parade, dignitaries and the general public went into the Pocahontas Theatre to hear Mr. Johnson's speech and his relayed greetings from the president. Daddy happened to be in the stage area following Johnson's presentation and said he heard very clearly Johnson's command to his military aide, "Get me out of this goddamn hellhole right now!"

Needless to say, Daddy never supported Lyndon Johnson and his Great Society. Bob Norris, Catherine Blevins, and some of Daddy's employees always joked that "Luke became a Republican soon after he made his first million." Daddy just couldn't abide the IRS and its tactics, high taxes, and unnecessary giveaway programs that were against his strong work ethics.

Chapter 60

At the End of the Hard Road

Northfork even had Christmas parades, and I would figure some way to ride in one of Daddy's convertibles and wave. I loved when Northfork city workers put up Christmas lights. The multicolored lights of red, yellow, green, and blue were big, round bulbs, much like the lights you might see in Italy.

It was a cold Christmas my senior year, but the family had a great holiday with Martha and her family, along with Remmie. It snowed New Year's Eve so Jimmy C. just came over, and Mother let us toast in the New Year with a glass of champagne. We would have one more Christmas with Remmie, and this was my last Christmas home before I headed out into another world. At that time, I just felt this holiday was special.

"Senioritis" hit us hard by April 1964, just like our new attention to the British invasion, The Beatles. We were counting the days until the prom, until we got our yearbooks, and until graduation. Jimmy C. and I double-dated with Fostina and her boyfriend Joe Taylor for the May 8 prom. With the theme "Bon Voyage," the juniors transformed half the gym into a cruise ship. I wore a pretty, yellow, Jackie Kennedy-type dress with a long, straight skirt that had some fancy work at the top. Most of the girls wore a full ball gown, and we all felt really special. Jimmy C. worked for two days, washing and polishing his uncle Sam's 1963 Ford. Did it ever look good! Our parents even gave us permission to go to the Red Barn in Bluefield for a late dinner after the prom, and we got to stay out until two in the morning. Of course, Daddy was in the living room when I got home, pretending he was asleep.

Around this time, I got a telephone call out of the blue from Jimmy Frank, calling to invite me to his Welch prom. To sweeten the deal, his uncle would even let him use his new car. He continued to tell me that every girl in McDowell County would want to go to the Welch prom, as it was *the* event, and then I could show those Welch girls a thing or two. I really wanted to go, but I knew it would cause a big stink with Jimmy C. More importantly, I knew his mother and family would be disappointed in me. I thought about telling Jimmy C. my parents were making me go, but the bottom line was, if some girl had asked Jimmy C. to their prom, I would have hit the ceiling. I finally refused Jimmy Frank's invitation. Of course, he got mad at me and didn't speak to me for at least four years.

A popular jewelry trend at this time for us girls was getting charm bracelets. I got quite a few charms on a new bracelet for graduation, loved it, and always wiggled my arm to hear the charms jingle. My very first charm, which I have always treasured, was a gift from Remmie.

At church we had a May Day ceremony honoring the Virgin Mary. Claire Owrey, Theresa Miller, Mary Krulatz, Edith Delomas, and I wore our prom dresses, and Charlotte Kowaleski was the May queen. We also had a church graduation with the Powhatan and Kimball kids. We all wore our caps and gowns and got church diplomas after mass. Jimmy Frank—who ignored me—and my cousin Johnny wore their maroon robes to represent Welch colors, while our boys wore blue robes for N–E. All the girls wore white robes. We all hated to leave Father Ryan.

We were "at the end of the hard road" as Daddy would say. All that was predictable, all that was normal, and all that we knew was going to change. We had no idea of what and where life would lead us.

Chapter 61

Graduation Time

The high school gym was transformed in May with flower arrangements and rows of folding chairs, signaling our end-of-year activities. Just as it was when Martha graduated, before we marched to "Pomp and Circumstance," came Class Night. Since Martha's graduation, we had enhanced the night's activities. The junior and senior girls dressed up in their prom gowns, and the junior and senior boys wore their suits. We were ready for a fun night. The juniors walked two by two into the gym to music, holding garlands of spring flowers that made an archway. As the music continued, the seniors walked in underneath the archway. After the school choir sang "Moon River," we read our Class History and our Class Prophecy, reflecting a fictional look at the town of Northfork in the year 1974. While not one prediction reflected the reality and changes we all awaited, we all enjoyed hearing our names called for some imaginary accomplishment. Our Class Wills held all the traditional intents and items so reflective of our time. For example, "I, Butch Boyd, will the ability to wreck my father's car to Eugene Cassel as if he doesn't already have that ability." Another was, "I, Mack Cornett, will my position as head drummer to Larry Williams." Or, "I, Dreama Tote, will my title as Most Athletic to Linda Carson." Or my favorite, "I, Thomas Hancock, will to Jeff Zamberlain $1.25 for the haircut I failed to get."

Our next ceremony was our baccalaureate, the church service for seniors. Several ministers from the Northfork area gave advice, the school choir sang, and we all prayed, leaving everyone confident and determined to do our best. Today these baccalaureate services seem to be a part of Graduations-Of-the-Past with protests and objections to combining education and religion.

Graduation night was June 4, 1964. It was our last hurrah, our final step to the future. The whole graduation thing for me was rather bittersweet—bitter only because Mother was angry when I did not wear a gold cord around my neck to signify the Highest Honor or the High Honor graduation status. Even though I ranked fifth academically in my class, I didn't get that recognition because of the D in Algebra back in the ninth grade. It was still haunting me.

I did try to solve this dilemma the summer before my senior year. I went to Mr. Atkinson, the principal, to ask if I needed to go to summer school in Welch to retake Algebra, make up for the D, and therefore graduate with Honors. I was ready to spend time and money to enroll, but he said, "Jen-na Lou-u-u, you don't have to retake the class in order to graduate with Honors." So I listened to him, didn't go, and suffered Mother's ire. Mother should have been angry with him, not me, but then no one made waves about fairness—right or wrong. Authority figures prevailed during that era in Northfork, and the concept of fairness did not necessarily come to the foreground. But not many days before the graduation ceremony, Mr. Atkinson bought a new four-door Pontiac model from Daddy, so that sealed the case closed.

"Jenna Lou Gianato." Finally my named was called, and after I walked across the stage at graduation—wearing my robe, cap with tassel, and no gold cord—I shook hands with that same principal, but forgot to get my diploma. Calling "Jenna Lou Gianato," again, I had to return to the stage to get my precious, black leather folder with my official graduation seal. Again, Woodrow Helms said later to Daddy, "I knew Jenna Lou would somehow steal the show." A positive that night was knowing that our classmates had chosen my friend Judy "Most Likely To Succeed."

We seniors had all been crazy to graduate, but it came so quickly that we really did not realize we would not see many of our very favorite friends hardly ever again. Of our graduating class, I would guess twenty percent of us went on to college. Like myself, Clara Lambie was accepted to a women's college—Stratford, in Virginia. Most others went to Concord College, French's Beauty School, or McLain's Business School, all in Mercer County, and no more than fifty miles away.

There were no scholarships, no government aid, and no Pell Grants. Parents either saved for college costs or borrowed money from Northfork's First Clark Bank or the Keystone National Bank. No one I knew growing up inherited money from their grandparents or had trust funds. The only "scholarship" I can remember was the Northfork Kiwanis Club giving a $100 award at graduation to Charlie Hamer, our football star. Martha and I were able to go to college on funds that Daddy made financing automobiles on his own. Martha always said she was grateful for Lillian Burk, a lady customer whose newly purchased car Dad had financed. He used the interest from that financing to pay for her Concord College fees. Still, in 1959 these fees were less than $300 a semester, and I think that also included her class textbooks.

Some of the boys joined the service, but most of our class members moved out of the area to find employment and/or marriage. We were good kids who cared about each other, but were mostly naïve about the world. I believe that none of us really had any idea exactly what we would be able to accomplish or appreciated the good education we got from McDowell County Schools.

Chapter 62

New York and the World's Fair

Daddy went to New York City for the National Automobile Convention during the summer before I left for Virginia Intermont. He asked me to go because the 1964 World's Fair was under way. He said I could invite Fostina, and her Mother also approved. We girls packed our best high heels and outfits and headed for Charleston to catch the plane. We didn't shut up the three-hour trip to the airport. While getting our bags out of the car, Daddy forgot his reading glasses and only had his prescription sunglasses for the entire trip.

Since I had been in New York in 1961, I thought I knew everything about the city. I wanted to do some college shopping, so Daddy gave me cash and made me pin it inside my bra. Since I was used to stuffing my bra with Kleenex, that was not a problem! Fostina and I hopped in a taxi, and off we went to Macy's. We shopped and shopped. I bought some really classy clothes, including a brown, suede coat and several matching skirts and blazers-everything the girls at Virginia Intermont wore. I had all my clothes shipped back to West Virginia since I really splurged.

We went to the World's Fair several days, and we always took the subway. We dressed up in our high heels, just like every other female who dressed up for airplane trips, big events, and church during that time frame. Of course our feet hurt, but we had such a fantastic time it didn't matter. We each had two 11-x-14 pictures done by artists and put in big frames. Poor Daddy carried all four of them around the World's Fair! Daddy and I called Mother from a booth that we could sit in, both of us talking at the same time—and she could hear us both. The phone even had push buttons, the way of the future!

We went to Yankee Stadium and watched the Yankees' baseball game. We saw Mickey Mantle, Roger Maris, and all of that great team. All this time Daddy had to wear his sunglasses everywhere. At night in the restaurants we had to read him the menu since it was usually so dark he couldn't see them. Fostina and I ordered very expensive meals because he couldn't see the prices! While he was packing the night before we left, Daddy heard us out in the hotel hall, laughing and making noise. He came out in his pajamas and sunglasses, which we thought was even funnier, and made us go back to our rooms. We girls had raided the maid's closet, and were trying to stuff New York toilet paper into our suitcases. Daddy made us put every single roll of toilet paper back. I think we drove him crazy, but he did laugh a lot too.

On departure day, Fostina and I decided to get our hair done in the hotel beauty shop. Of course, we wanted it teased, and put up in a French twist, and this took time. With each of us having thick hair, it took forever. Daddy kept coming in, pacing the floor, and saying we had to go. In fact, he got quite upset that this took so long. We barely made it back to the airport in time to catch the flight to Charleston. The weather in Charleston was hot and sunny, and Daddy wanted to put the top down on the convertible he had driven. Of course we said no since we didn't want our "New York" hairdos to get all messed up before anyone in Northfork could see them. I specifically asked him to stop by the post office first because I knew word would get around about our hairdos. The whole trip was fun and very special. Daddy said he had a good time even though all we did was talk, talk, talk! Not long after our trip, Fostina's mother bought from Daddy a fully-equipped, white Pontiac Catalina convertible with a black top and black interior.

A few things I didn't get for college in New York, I purchased at a nice ladies' shop in Northfork—The Quality Shop—more commonly known as Chris's. The owner and every sales person smoked. They had a nice sectional couch and all the ladies would come in, sit, gossip, smoke, and buy clothes. Chris had a suit club. The customer paid five dollars a week toward the suit club. A drawing was held once a month, and the winner got a new suit. Those not winning got credit toward a new suit when they purchased one. I can't imagine that everything in the store didn't smell like smoke, but then again, everyone smoked. All the ladies seemed to think it was a good idea that I was going to the high-class Virginia Intermont.

Chapter 63

Father Ryan's Big Surprise

A few weeks before I left for college, Father Ryan called the house. Mother answered. He asked if I could come up to the rectory and do some typing for him because he had some major paperwork with three carbon copies that had to go to the bishop in Wheeling. She thought it was odd, rolled her eyes, but said OK. I had never been in the rectory and was somewhat taken aback, but felt honored he wanted me to help him out.

When I arrived, he asked me to take a seat. He said that he really didn't have any typing for me to do. I immediately thought he had heard about something I'd done wrong. Father Ryan said he had something to tell me. He said he wanted me to know something since I was going away to college. He said things may change in my home because I was leaving. Father Ryan proceeded to tell me that one of the parishioners told him Daddy was going to ask Mother for a divorce after I went to college, and then he was going to marry her.

You have to understand that Martha and I learned the word divorce before we understood the word marriage. We had heard from Mother, "we are staying together for the girls," so many times we were immune to all the arguments about leaving and divorce through the years. I wasn't exactly in shock. While visibly shaken, I wasn't surprised. I heard from friends who lived near the woman that they were an item. I couldn't understand his attraction, but assumed she treated him well. Of course, I could understand her attraction due to his personality, his manner, and perhaps his money. After I left the rectory, I knew I couldn't go straight home since Mother would know I had been crying, so I went by Martha's house and told her. We were in the same boat with this information, and we both tried to shake it off. We had heard similar scenarios many times.

Chapter 64

And So It Goes

In early September 1964, I packed up those wonderful clothes from New York in my red Samonsite luggage and in the red footlocker I ordered from Budnick's in Keystone ("Drive a Little, Save A Lot"). I even had a matching, red, Royal manual typewriter. I then headed for the biggest change of my life, college!

I thought of how we were different than most of the folks growing up in the coalfields and Appalachia from the time I was a young girl until I went to college. We had some neat experiences.

I got a telegram from Santa Claus, and Mother pinned it to my Christmas stocking. We got clothes from New York when Daddy went to the World Series, and we all wore corsages at Easter. Color was important to the people, places, and things in our lives when we grew up. For Mother's Day we would all get dressed up and put on carnation corsages. You wore the color red if your mother was alive, white if your mother was dead. One year Aunt Gladys, Remmie, Mother, Martha, and I all had red corsages. Poor Daddy had a single white one in his lapel. On that Mother's Day, the women wore fur pieces, hats, gloves, and all their finery. We went to dinner in Bluefield and then stopped at Pinnacle Rock and took pictures. Nobody else did that.

We did color Easter eggs and have baskets, but every year we also got colored chickens or ducks. G.C. Murphy Five and Dime Store sold live chicks or ducklings dyed blue, green, and red. We usually got three of them, one in each color. As the chicks or ducklings grew, the color disappeared. Usually they either died or "something" killed them, since they stayed outside.

Mother had the dealership's body shop spray her Christmas trees every year. Everyone had green trees. We had white or silver. I assume we had no idea of the toxic fumes the paint from the tree put out, but there was a lot of cigarette smoke around the house so we never smelled it. The exception was the year Mother purchased an aluminum tree. You didn't have to put up lights. It had a revolving spotlight that lit the tree in colors changing from green, red, or blue.

Daddy was one of the first to get a Polaroid camera. He could take a photo, tear it off, apply a solution, and then let it dry. It seemed like we had a lot of photos that looked yellow. But it was cool to see the photo appear after a minute or two. Martha and I won't forget the summer we were at Myrtle Beach in ninety degree heat and hot sun. People really stared and pointed at us when we rode by in our 1957 red and white Pontiac with all the windows up. Air-conditioning in automobiles was a new concept, and we thought we were special. Who else had their family portrait done at the Greenbrier? Family portraits weren't even heard of, much less at the Greenbrier. Who else but me had a subscription to *Little Lulu* or *Millie the Model* funny books? These came through the mail and Mamie, the postmistress, would always say, "Jenna Lou, your *Little Lulu* is here."

Because of the dealership, we always had window scrapers, plastic hair bonnets, ashtrays, and matches with "Gianato Pontiac" advertising on them—even after the new-car showing. Daddy gave away items like Rodney Dangerfield did pencils in the *Back to School* movie. If someone was really special, he might get the latest proof set of coins. The Kennedy coins were particularly special. No one else's dad read the *Wall Street Journal* or books about being positive, salesmanship, or how to make money. Daddy named Mother, Martha, and me as directors and officers of his corporations, allowing us to receive profit-sharing dividends throughout the years. But that was the stuff that made us feel special when things didn't go so well in other areas of our lives.

Time moved on. Daddy's dealership grew and the business prospered, not only in Northfork but also in Welch. Mother finally got her peace and quiet and took up golf. Martha became a successful West Virginia educator with a wonderful husband, Don, who was an industry leader in coal mining training and safety. Her daughter, Laura, became an educator teaching biology, physics, and chemistry. She and her husband, Mark, have two children. I left behind my teaching job in Yorktown, Virginia when Jim accepted a position with FedEx in Memphis. With the opportunities that FedEx offered for women, I worked my way up the ladder in positions I never dreamed possible way back in 1964. Retiring on the same day, Jim and I travel, play golf, and still love games of chance. Our daughter, Jennifer, and her husband, Michael, are both with United Airlines, and Jennifer travels worldwide as a flight attendant. Mother and Daddy stayed married and together until his death in 1996. My parents' relationship had a profound effect on Martha and me, although we were in denial for years. In years to come, we would look for security and predictability in relationships and learn that "staying together for the girls" was not always the healthy remedy to marriage. We had good times, sad times, and changing times—some predictable, some not.

Northfork was like many towns. We had the successful, the failures, the kind, and the gossips. We had the dirty old men, the straightlaced, the cheats, and those who were scorned. Yet, underneath this small-town façade of positives and negatives, we girls also saw those who lived with broken promises and disappointments. Northfork was a town that shaped us all; and we will always remember those years in the middle of the twentieth century in that little McDowell County community.

So I guess in Northfork there were big fish, little fish, and those who just swam around. Even though the town was small, all my favorite fish were big to me. No doubt, above all, to those folks in Northfork when we were growing up, Martha and I will always be remembered as "Luke's Daughters."

The four of us pose for a family photo. Pictured are Luke, Jenny, and "Luke's Daughters," Martha and Jenna Lou.

ACKNOWLEDGMENTS

Jim Calovini for his love and encouragement, believing our story was worth telling, spelling expertise, and laughing when he was supposed to laugh.

Don Rector for his love and interest, coal mining expertise, and believing we would finish.

Jennifer Harris Somogyi for believing we could do this project, and being excited as we passed milestones.

Laura Hurst Jaworski for her encouragement as we recounted our early years in the coalfields, leaving this historical footprint for her children.

Judy Helms Sargent for shared memories, photos, the 1964 Class History, Class Will, and Class Prophecy, great editing ideas, encouragement, and friendship.

Clara Lambie Keesee Fry for her friendship, encouragement, positive feedback, suggestions, and shared memories.

Bonnie McKeever for her interest, good insight to the project, editing, and ideas about the times.

Kay Moody for her help in editing, expertise in all technical work, and positive feedback.

Ginger Hawkins, Kacey Hissam Moore, Sherry McCraw, Nancy Wilson Hames, Doris Boyd, Frances Wingfield, and Jeane Fullen for their thoughts, encouragement, and ideas.

Roland Jaworski, Kayleah Jaworski, and Jayce Robinson for giving us ideas, really reading what we had to say, and asking all the right questions.

Richie Norcia for his specific suggestions, printing expertise, and input for the front and back covers.

Special thanks to CreateSpace for editing our book and to the CreateSpace Project Team 5 for their expertise with our interior and exterior design, and their professional guidance during the developmental process.

Contact Authors: lukesdaughters@yahoo.com

Made in the USA
Monee, IL
23 February 2021